UNLOCKING
Y O U R
POTENTIAL

UNLOCKING
Y O U R
POTENTIAL

Winning Your Inner Struggles

H A R O L D [J.] S A L A

VISION™
HOUSE
PUBLISHING, INC.
Gresham, Oregon 97030

JUL 9 8

Published by Vision House Publishing, Inc.
1217 NE Burnside, Suite 403
Gresham, Oregon 97030

Edited by Chip MacGregor

Printed in the United States of America

International Standard Book Number: 1-885305-46-x

Unless otherwise indicated, all Scripture references are from the
New International Version of the Bible, The Lockman Foundation
© 1960, 1962, 1963, 1968, 1971, 1972, 1973, 1975, 1977.
Used by permission.

96 97 98 99 00 01 02 03 04 05 — 10 9 8 7 6 5 4 3 2 1

In memory of my father,
whose example to me as I was growing up
gave me the confidence that I could do what
God wanted me to accomplish!

Chapter Nine

Coping With Stress 161

Chapter Ten

Burn-Out: Terminal Stress 183

A Final Word

Pogo, a popular comic strip character, and his friends decide to wage war against an unspecified foe. They go forth against the enemy with their swords drawn, their spears readied. With lines of grim determination written on their faces, they are ready to attack.

Then the cartoonist pictures Pogo and his friends returning from the battle, which didn't take place, discouraged, and disillusioned. The swords are sheathed, their spears dragging in the dust behind them. The caption reads: "We have met the enemy, and he is us!"

What Pogo discovered is exactly what I, sometimes painfully, have learned about myself! The greatest enemies are not the ones out there lurking in the dark. They are within!

The greatest struggles in life are not fought on the battle fields of the world; they are fought in human hearts as we struggle with forces within: fear, worry, inadequacies, feelings of inferiority, anger, frustration, stress, and the inability to cope with the circumstances which are not to our liking.

While these challenges can destroy you—as they do many people, or they at least reduce the person's effectiveness in life and his level of fulfillment and happiness—they can also serve as a catalyst to bring out the best in you.

Unlocking Your Potential is written with this purpose in mind. None of us chooses the circumstances or the time of his birth, but we do make choices as to how we respond to the circumstances of life. In this book, I haven't attempted to define all of our inner struggles from the perspective of psychology or *what's out there* in the marketplace. Rather, I have taken a look at some of the most troubling issues that we struggle with from a biblical perspective, striving to see how God views these issues. Then, I help apply the spiritual guidelines of the Bible to these needs. Scripture quotations are from the New International Bible unless otherwise indicated.

May God help you to win those inner struggles and be a better, a more fulfilled person as the result of it.

Harold J. Sala
Mission Viejo, California

CHAPTER ONE

Understanding Yourself

You're worth the bother

Have you ever done something—either without really thinking about it or possibly even with a great deal of forethought—and then later scratched your head as you asked yourself, "What in the world possessed me to do that?" Or, "Why did I do such a thing? I really knew better!"

At the time, under those circumstances, you did what you thought was the right thing. Perhaps, in trying to avoid personal responsibility for what you were doing, you reasoned, "Everybody is doing it," or you may have even thought, "Surely God wouldn't want me to be lonely!"

Later, you looked back and regretted the decision that you made. I'm not suggesting for a moment that you go about as an amateur psychiatrist psychoanalyzing yourself, second-guessing your decisions. What I am saying is that the better you understand yourself the greater the measure of happiness and fulfillment you will have in life.

Loneliness, anger, frustration, stress, peer-pressure, passions, and the desire to please both man and God are all factors in your behavior. The more you know what makes you tick, the more you will be in control of your life.

Socrates was credited with the simple maxim: KNOW THYSELF. The wise man of Athens taught his disciples that a knowledge of self was prerequisite to a deep understanding of life. But Socrates wasn't the first to look within his heart, and ponder the mystery of life and what makes us behave as we do.

At least six centuries before Socrates, a wiser man, David, King of Israel, pondered the nature of man. He wrote, "When I consider your heavens, the work of your fingers, the moon and the stars, which you have set in place, what is man that you are mindful of him, the son of man that you care for him?" (Psalm 8:3,4). David wasn't the only writer of Scripture who contemplated the complexity of man's nature in an attempt to understand himself. The Old Testament book of Proverbs is a collection of wisdom literature compiled about the time of Solomon, and in this book there is an underlying theme of man's attempt to discover his true nature.

More recently, psychology, as one of the branches of behavioral science, has delved into the mind of man to help us understand our behavior better. The word psychology comes from two Greek words, psuche meaning *soul* and logos meaning *a word* or *the study of.* Hence, modern psychology is the study of man's nature and behavior. The study of psychology does provide certain insights in understanding ourselves, but an even deeper understanding of ourselves and our natures comes through God's textbook on life and living—the Bible, which came through the inspiration of the Holy Spirit.

Is it worth the time and effort to try to understand our-selves and the pressures and forces that contribute to our behavior? Indeed, it is! For example, if you are a parent—married or single—with needs in your life which are not met, in all probability you will be frustrated. That frustration may well contribute to your having relationships and getting involved in situations which are not in your best interest. Furthermore, if you do not understand what your needs are and how to meet them, your children may grow up with blind spots in their own lives. Understanding yourself is the first step toward being a better parent.

You Are A Unique Individual–An Original Without Duplication

Today we hear a lot about *rugged individualism*. But when it gets down to the bottom line, most of us are not rugged individualists at all; we are pressure-cooked into bland uniformity with everyone else. We tend to think of individualism as something quaint or odd rather than something which is beautiful, right, and good.

God made you an individual. In these days of *mass everything,* we seem to have lost sight of the fact that individuality resulted from God's design. A unique arrangement of genes and chromosomes, established at conception, makes each of us unique. The three trillion cells in your body are put together just a bit differently than they are in all of the other 5 billion people here on earth.

Seldom do we ever think about the marvelous complexity of our bodies. Few people realize how many and how compli-cated are the systems that function within our bodies. Every seven years, your body replaces its three trillion cells with new ones, a process that gradually slows as you age. Your brain is an amazing organ that serves as the nerve center of your body. Should you have the misfortune of sitting on a tack, a message to your brain is immediately transmitted via a network of nerves. Your brain, in turn, formulates an expression of pain that your vocal chords express in no uncertain terms. All of this takes place almost instantaneously.

Yale University psychologist Dr. Neal Miller describes the human brain as the most complex organism on earth. It contains 100 billion cells or neurons, and each of these is connected with 10,000 billion other nerves by fibers.[1]

Your body has an amazing air conditioning system that adjusts to your environment. Your skin has more than 2 million tiny sweat glands on its surface—about 300 per square inch—that are regulated to keep your body at an even temperature.

Your heart, slightly larger than a man's fist, pumps blood through your veins and arteries. In your stomach are 35 million glands secreting juices to aid the process of digestion—acids strong enough to take varnish off a table, yet working harmlessly in your body.

All of this we take for granted. Never do we have to say, "Brain cell number 222,334, get to work; you aren't carrying your load."

Now, see how this applies to you as an individual. Nobody thinks with your mind or reasons exactly as you do; neither does anyone see with your eyes or hear with your ears, walk with your legs or hold things with your hands. No one else in all the world feels what you feel. You are one of a kind, without duplication.

Your vantage point is different from everyone else in our world. There is tremendous freedom in accepting the fact that you don't have to be pressured into conformity with everybody else. You can be yourself, an individual created in the image of God with sensitivity and personality that came from His design.

A retired army officer, the father of twelve children—six sons and six daughters—told me about his children and how no two were exactly alike. "Each one," he reflected, "is different from the rest. Though they are alike in some ways, when you consider them individually, each is unlike any other."

Diamonds, emeralds, and rubies are all precious stones, yet they have properties and characteristics that make them unique and different. No two diamonds are exactly alike. Their color, cut, and clarity all define them. So it is with individual differences in a family. Two children may have the same parents, be raised in the same family, and even share friends in common, yet those two may be vastly unlike each other in many ways.

Today we badly need to understand that it's O.K. to be yourself, an individual created in the image of God with gifts and talents that no one else has in exactly the same mix.

You Are A Spiritual Being

The second fact that will help you to understand yourself is to recognize that you are an individual who has a spiritual nature. This is one area where much of modern psychology and psychiatry has had a blind spot. Many psychologists and psychiatrists don't recognize that man is anything more than a highly developed mammal. Rather, he is essentially a spiritual being made in the image of God and, therefore, he has a spiritual nature.

The Bible says that it is your spiritual and moral nature that sets you apart from lower forms of life. But, when you lose sight of that spiritual nature, your conduct may well take on characteristics of those who live as though there is no God and no accounting for our actions to Him.

Down through the centuries men and women, in different ways, have described the barrenness of an empty life that comes when the spiritual nature of our lives is ignored. Augustine, in the Fourth Century, wrote that the human heart is restless until it finds itself in God. Rene Paschal, the French philosopher, described that yearning for fulfillment and wholeness as a *God-shaped vacuum* in the heart of every person that can be filled only by Jesus Christ.

If you really want to understand yourself, realize that you're not a highly evolved animal; rather, you are a human being who has complex emotional and spiritual needs that cannot be separated into neat compartments. Your emotions affect your spiritual life. In turn, your spiritual life powerfully affects your sense of right and wrong, your feelings of guilt or compliance with the will of God.

The entire story of redemption is actually a very simple one. It is the story of how sin or rebellion estranged man from his creator, and of how a loving Father sent His Son to bridge the gulf between us and God, and to bring us back into fellowship with Him. Isaiah, the prophet of old, put it, "We all, like sheep, have gone astray, each of us has turned to his own way" (Isaiah 53:6a).

The fact that something happened to our spiritual life back with our first father Adam explains a lot of things in the world. It explains how a Hitler could send fourteen million people—six million Jews and eight million Gentiles—to their deaths in the concentration camps of Europe. But it also explains a great deal about life today, and even your personal life, things that you would prefer to ignore, or at least minimize.

It explains how a husband can be unfaithful to a wife who dearly loves him, and visa versa. It explains how we all find ourselves doing things at times that we know are wrong, but enjoying them anyway.

Paul talked about this conflict in our natures when he wrote Romans chapter seven. You can probably identify with him: "I don't understand myself at all, for I really want to do what is right, but I can't. I do what I don't want to do—what I hate. I know perfectly well that what I am doing is wrong, and my bad conscience proves that I agree with these laws I am breaking" (Romans 7:15,16, Living Bible). Paul is saying that the very things he didn't want to do were the things that he did, and the very things he did want to do were the things which were left undone. He sounded out the despair of a lot of people when he wrote, "What a wretched man that I am! Who will rescue me from this body of death?" (Romans 7:24).

That's part of the reason that at times you are torn between doing things you know will hurt yourself or another person, and doing what is right. You feel incapable of helping yourself and you begin to resent yourself and wish that you were different. In that same passage, Paul says that you can be different because of the power of God's Holy Spirit; he writes in Romans 8:1, "Therefore, there is now no condemnation for those who are in Christ Jesus."

As a believer, you can stand in the presence of God, justified or free of the guilt of your sins because you have been forgiven. Paul put it like this: "God made him [Christ] who had no sin to be sin for us, so that in him we might become the righteousness of God" (2 Corinthians 5:21).

It doesn't mean, however, that the age-old struggle of the flesh and the Spirit will not be with you until the end of time. It will. The difference is that, as God's child, there comes an enabling that makes it possible for you to live in such a way that you are in harmony with God's will. This is the power of Christ within you.

The mentality of our day is that God expects far too much of us, more than we are capable of delivering. In other words, He doesn't really mean what He says. But the Good News of the Gospel is that your life can be different, enriched, and enabled because of God's indwelling power.

You Are A Person Of Great Value

May I ask you a personal question? Do you like yourself? Or secretly—or maybe not so secretly—would you like to be someone else? Why don't you like yourself? There are a variety of reasons to choose from: You can say...

I don't like the way I look.

I don't like my figure.

I'm just a nobody.

I'm not as gifted as some.

My personality isn't as good as so-and-so.

I don't have the brains that he has.

I can't think of clever things to say.

There is no limit to the extent to which you can be unhappy with yourself if you really try.

A listener to my radio program, Guidelines for Family Living, wrote the following: "I have a sister who is very petite and flat-chested and this upsets her very much. She can't accept the fact that there are a lot more pretty clothes for small women than for big women. Her husband loves her very much and so do her children, but she has this hang-up about her body."

Women are not the only ones who are unhappy with themselves. Quite typical is the way one man described himself:

"I am a disabled man with a spine disorder...always living in pain and weakness. Sometimes, I wonder why the Lord lets me suffer and endure this kind of life. I am ridiculed and mocked by others due to my ugly figure. No one really understands me, not even my wife."

X When you are not happy with yourself, you won't be happy with others. You will see in them the faults that you resent in yourself, and you will transfer your dislike to others. And when you are not happy with yourself, you're not happy with God either. You reason, "He made me like I am; so it is really His fault that I am like I am."

As I write this I'm thinking of a teenage girl who attempted to take her life on a couple of occasions. She wasn't very pretty, and it was obvious that she not only hated herself, she disliked almost everybody else too: her parents, her teachers, and most of her contemporaries. About the only friends that she had were a few disgruntled teenagers who were very much like herself. Alcohol, drugs, and sex were all trips that she had taken to try to find some meaning to the puzzle of life.

Today, she is a different person because she came face to face with the fact that our rebellion against ourselves is really rebellion against God. We are the only ones who can respond to His love and cooperate with Him in making ourselves what we ought to be.

In the last decade, plastic surgery has preyed on this weakness in our thinking, that self-worth comes through a more beautiful body. Take out those wrinkles, get rid of that excess fat, enlarge your breasts, make yourself attractive to members of the opposite sex. And we bought into this mentality, spending hundred of millions to pay for surgical procedures that were cosmetic. Now we have begun to realize that the procedures may boomerang on us, producing a fall-out of hideous consequences.

Do Yourself A Favor—Love Yourself

Is it really wrong to have a measure of love for yourself? You have probably been taught that in order to love others you must denigrate yourself and crucify your flesh. You are right that we are to love one another (John 13:34, 1 John 4:7,8). Jesus said very plainly that one of the hallmarks of Christianity is the love that believers have for each other, a love unlike that of individuals who do not know Christ. This love results from the Holy Spirit's indwelling presence in our lives. However, one of the reasons that God's love doesn't flow through some individuals to anyone else is that it is bottled up by feelings ranging from a mild dislike to hatred for themselves.

Paul says that we ought not to think of ourselves more highly than is proper (Romans 12:3), but the inverse truth is just as meaningful: if you think of yourself less highly than is proper, you are just as wrong.

Then what of Jesus' statement that we are to love our neighbor as ourselves (see Matthew 22:39)? In saying this, Jesus recognized that an understanding of who you are and a recognition of your gifts and abilities brings a security that comes from within. It is essential if you are ever to learn to love your neighbor. The amount of hatred that we see today is evidence that we have never learned to love ourselves.

Even so, the concept of loving our neighbor as ourselves didn't originate in the Gospels. Long before, Moses faithfully recorded God's command: "Do not seek revenge or bear a grudge against one of your people, but love your neighbor as yourself" (Leviticus 19:18).

If you don't learn to love yourself, you will never be very successful loving anyone else. As Soren Kierkegaard put it:

"When the commandment to love one's neighbor is rightly understood, it also says the converse, 'Thou shalt love thyself in the right way.' If anyone, therefore, will not learn from Christianity to love himself in the right way, then neither can he love his neighbor.... To love one's self in the right way, and to love one's neighbor, are absolutely analogous concepts, and are at the bottom one and the same."[2]

In his book, *Peace Of Mind,* Joshua Liebman went even further in recognizing the impossibility of loving others when negative feelings of self-dislike or hate are present:

"He who hates himself, who does not have a proper regard for his own capacities... can have no respect for others. Deep within himself, he will hate his brothers when he sees in them his own marred image. Love for oneself is the foundation of a brotherly society and personal peace of mind."[3]

Your ability to love is vitally affected by the way you think about yourself. I'm thinking of individuals I have worked with who told me how their parents had cursed them and berated them with deprecating labels like, "You're no good!" "You've got bad blood in you!" or, "You're the dumbest kid in our family!" And the youngster began to visualize himself or herself as a loser, a person of little value. What self-confidence there was quickly began to erode and eventually those harsh words became a self-fulfilling prophecy.

God knows that all of us wrestle with enough of those feelings without having them hammered into our heads. To realize, however, that you can change with God's help, that you don't have to live in a prison of inadequacy and inferiority, that you don't have to let circumstances destroy your future, is the first step toward becoming the kind of person you think God wants you to be and that you would like to become.

You Are Capable Of Change

First, let me point out that a lot of people take refuge in failure situations. It is far easier for them to feel sorry for themselves and cry over their misery than it is for them to assume a responsible plan of change. Year after year, they tell other people about their difficulties and their failures. They are like walking clouds of gloom and doom, ready to tell you how they have been victimized by life. They'll tell you how their husband walked out and left them with nine children, and that they are absolutely helpless to help themselves because of the misfortunes that befell them. And you know something—they convince themselves! They take real delight in recounting the sordid details of their misery. Don't be one of them!

William Glasser is a psychiatrist who broke with the traditional approach to psychotherapy. In doing so, he developed an approach to the treatment of mental problems that is quite consistent with what Scripture says about the effects of our failures. Glasser says that the past doesn't have to destroy our future. In fact, he refuses to listen to the sordid details of people's failures. He uses the term "psychiatric garbage" to describe the endless recounting of our troubles. Rather, Glasser focuses on the fact that a lot of people suffer from "paralysis of analysis," as he describes it. They are doing nothing to change their lives and they want nothing done, but they are willing to spend endless hours talking about how they got into trouble. Talk is cheap, and a lot easier than working to bring change.

Let me summarize by saying that if you are to change your life and the circumstances, three things are necessary: First, the desire to change; second, a commitment to change; and finally, follow-through. Change involves the cooperation of man and God, your working with the Divine in working out His will for your life. Try to do everything in your own strength and you won't get very far, for you will very soon discover the weakness of human resolutions and good intentions. A lot of others before you, perhaps some even stronger than you are, have tried to turn over the *new leaf.* Their attempt at reformation resulted in producing another soiled page in the book of their life.

When it comes to personality and behavioral change, the Holy Spirit is the greatest force in all the world. He who works in the life of the believer to bring him into conformity with God's plan and purpose; but, this change or power is activated only by man's complete cooperation with the Divine. An individual's determination to stay in the prison of self-pity or despair short-circuits the restorative work of the Holy Spirit.

Do you fully believe that you can be different? Instead of being angry with the world that you aren't six inches taller, you can work in harmony with the Holy Spirit to develop the kind of personality that lifts you six inches higher. Instead of cursing God and blaming the economy for your financial difficulty, with God's help you can begin to formulate a plan on how to break out of your economic woes, trusting God for wisdom and guidance.

One more thing needs to be said in this chapter. Many people were disadvantaged by growing up in homes where they were neglected or abused, or they have had certain failures in life that have stunted their development. If this fits you, you need to know that the longer you live with a failure situation, the more difficult it becomes to break out of the pattern of negative thinking that has imprisoned you. The longer you live with negative situations, the more comfortable you become with them and the more effectively they ensnare you.

Once you determine that your life can be different, you must make peace with yourself. The next chapter shows you how to accept yourself as you understand your true value and worth. Remember, you are your own worst enemy.

Discussion Questions:

A couple got into a heated argument. Finally, in frustration, the husband said, "I don't understand why God made you so beautiful and so dumb at the same time!" Without batting an eyelash, she fired back, "That's easy! God made me beautiful so you would love me; He made me dumb so I would love you!" This is a woman who knew who she was and why!

1. Humor aside, what affect would her husband's words have had on her if the wife really believed that she was dumb? How might she work to overcome those insecurities?

2. What are two negative opinions you used to have of yourself that are no longer true, at least to the degree that they used to be? How did you learn to decrease the effect they have on your life?

3. What are two negative characteristics that you still see at work in your life? Try to take a clear, objective look at yourself. In what ways, if any, are you choosing to stay *stuck?* What are three ways you can take action to change those characteristics or opinions?

4. To *love* yourself, according to Scripture, is to take care of yourself physically, emotionally, and spiritually so that you have something to give to others. What is one way you can take care of yourself in each of those areas today?

This will hurt....

We are more likely to react that to respond when someone says something negative about us, especially when that person is an important part of our lives. There are two reactions that are hurtful—either to yourself or to the other person.

First, you might simply believe what the other person has said, and use that as fuel in the fire of self-degradation. Your habit might be to simply accept what other people say, and beat yourself up for being that way. There is little motivation to change if you don't believe it's possible.

The second hurtful reaction is to lash out—maybe with angry words, maybe with complete denial. Some people refuse to see that they have any problems at all. Deep inside, though, they feel the punches, and they harbor the hurt.

Either reaction will always compound your feelings of insecurity.

This will help...

Someone once told Abraham Lincoln that one of his generals called him a fool. He replied, "Well, then, I must be one, because he is almost always right."

When you are hit with a criticism, it will help to stop a moment and consider that the person might have a point. You build the security to do this when you know that, as God's child, He sees you as a person of infinite value and worth. If what the person who made the *dig* said has even the smallest bit of truth to it, this might be motivation for you to work on that area of life. But if you have taken an honest look at yourself and you know that he is way off base, let it go. It is not worth the cost, to yourself or to the relationship, of reacting.

Notes

[1]David Ferrell, "The Brain: An Inner Universe," *The Orange County Register,* July 1983, sec. J, p. 1l. For further information see Neil Miller, "Start at the Top: The Brain Is Our Giant Data Base," The Orange County Register, June 12, 1985, sec. D, p. 1.

[2]Soren Kierkegaard, *Works of Love* trans. by David Swenson as quoted by Cecil Osborn in The Art of Understanding Yourself, p. 217.

[3]Joshua Liebman, *Peace of Mind,* p. 71.

CHAPTER TWO

Answering The Question:

Who am I?

A television station sent a reporter and crew out on the street to interview people. The reporter asked but one question, "Who are you?" In order to make the research valid, each person was asked to give the first three answers that came to mind. Then, the psychological and social implications of the answers were evaluated.

If an individual replied, "I'm a man!" or "I'm a woman!" that individual was thought to be conscious of his or her sexual identity.

If a woman answered, "Oh, I'm just a housewife," researchers concluded that she was unaware of the importance of her role as a wife and mother.

If a man replied, "I'm an executive, a stockholder, and a family man," it was believed that he was aware of his position in life, his social status, and his marital obligations.

Now, if you were walking down the mall and a reporter from a local television station put a microphone in front of your face and asked, "Who are you?" how would you answer?

There is a problem with identity in today's society. Nearly every women's magazine on the newsstand has an article or two about discovering your identity. I hasten to add that women aren't the only ones faced with this problem. Vast numbers of men, especially those who have been highly paid executives, suddenly find their image compromised when they are suddenly laid off. They no longer don pricey business suits, and commute to the office with a highly polished leather briefcase in hand. No. They stay at home. They scour the want ads. They hesitantly apply for unemployment. They are no longer major contributors to the family's income, and they face an identity crisis of major proportions. If one of these men was asked, "Who are you?" he would be uncertain how to answer. "I used to be..." would not be an uncommon answer.

When we lack a clearly defined sense of identity, we feel inadequate, uncertain, and insecure. This can lead to one of two extremes. On one hand, feelings of inadequacy lead to an *inferiority complex*. On the other hand, they may cause an individual to push too hard. This overcompensation produces a *superiority complex*. He or she tries to demonstrate—or might even tell other people outright—how good he or she really is. But if you really are good, you don't have to tell people. They know!

One of the primary reasons that we have difficulty in accepting ourselves and having a positive mental image of ourselves is that we do not understand how important we are in the sight of God. When we fail to sense our importance to Him, that feeling of unimportance eventually trickles down into every part of our lives, until we consider ourselves to be of little, if any, practical value. We feel shame at our deficiency as a human being, and that results in feelings of inferiority and inadequacy.

Have you ever asked yourself, "How does God look at my life? Am I important to Him at all, or does what happens to me really make any difference to Him?" The next logical question after that is, "Then how important am I to Him anyway?"

In His ministry, Jesus never lost sight of the importance of a single person, no matter how lowly or insignificant that individual's position seemed in life. In fact, some of His most profound theological discourses came as the result of conversations that he had with individuals who were considered rather unimportant by society at large.

Consider the importance of what Jesus said about His Father's will, following a conversation at the well of Sychar with a woman who was a social outcast. At the time, the disciples were astonished. Not only did Jesus talk to a woman, but that woman was also a Samaritan. In all probability, she was a woman of ill-repute, since she drew water at high noon; *virtuous* women came to draw water either early in the day or late in the afternoon (see John 4).

And what of the beautiful passage stressing forgiveness, which came from Jesus' encounter with an adulterous woman—a woman seized in the very act? Instead of reaching for a stone, Jesus extended compassion and forgiveness. "Go now and leave your life of sin" was His direction (see John 8:1-11).

When Jesus dealt with individuals, He looked beyond the veneer that produces social isolation and peer groups which refuse to cross ethnic and social barriers. He disregarded custom and tradition. He saw value in each person with whom He came in contact—something that greatly distressed the Pharisees.

You Are A Person Of Worth And Value In God's Sight

Jesus' attitude toward the individual was but a reflection of His Father's attitude, revealed in the pages of the Old Testament and amplified by the writings of the New Testament.

In particular, the Apostle Paul gave insights about an individual's worth when he wrote to the Ephesians. He stressed that it was the sacrifice of Christ that enabled God not only to forgive us, but to accept us and receive us as His adopted children.

In the first few paragraphs of the Ephesian letter, he stressed several facts regarding the believer.

1. God has chosen us before creation (Ephesians 1:4).

2. God has adopted us into His family (Ephesians 1:5).

3. God has accepted us in Christ (Ephesians 1:6).

4. God has forgiven us because of the blood that was shed (Ephesians 1:7).

It is my belief, based on counseling and working with thousands of men and women over the years, that an understanding of these simple truths is necessary if you are to understand your value and worth in God's sight. The key to self-acceptance is knowing and believing that God accepts you on the basis of what Jesus did for you. Especially helpful is the King James translation of Ephesians 1:6, which says, "He [God] has made us accepted in the beloved [Christ]."

In life in our society, acceptance is based largely on three factors: appearance, performance and influence. You only have to go to a department store to see that appearance is important.

34

Notice who gets waited on first when an elderly, slightly over-weight woman and a young, vivacious, very pretty woman are both waiting for a sales person. Performance is also the basis of acceptance in many situations. It is the student who has performed with the highest grades who is admitted to the best college. And the influence of a father with the right connections can sometimes get a young man appointed to a team before the one with the best overall record is accepted.

This is *the way it is.* But, unlike what we have come to accept as the way it is, the Bible teaches that acceptance with God is never based on your appearance, performance, or influence, neither negatively or positively. Because we generally believe that God is good, we tend to think that if we are good enough He will be impressed and accept us. Actually, your essential goodness, or your lack of it, has nothing to do with God accepting you. "He saved us, not because of righteous things we had done, but because of his mercy. He saved us through the washing of rebirth and renewal by the Holy Spirit" (Titus 3:5).

The Gospel is Good News because it proclaims that no self-improvement program is necessary before you can come to the Father for forgiveness and help. Scores of individuals, however, are crippled emotionally by the popular belief that God accepts only those who are good enough. They believe that, at the end of the trip, God draws a line. If your good deeds out-number the bad, then and only then will He receive you and forgive you.

When your concept of God's forgiveness is deficient, you can never fully accept the truth that God has forgiven you. And when you are uncertain of your relationship with Him, you will find it difficult or even impossible to forgive yourself as well.

Understanding God's point of view, that the blood of Christ was shed enabling God to accept us and forgive us, is essential to understanding and accepting yourself.

Because God loves you, you can love yourself.

Because God cares about you, you must care about yourself.

Because God has forgiven you, you must forgive yourself.

Because God has accepted you, you must learn to accept yourself.

Perhaps the following diagram will help you to better understand this concept:

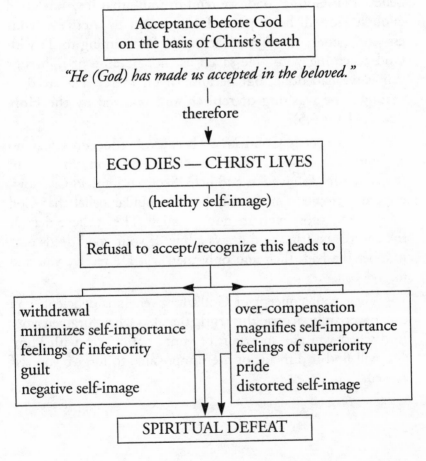

Acceptance before God
on the basis of Christ's death

"He (God) has made us accepted in the beloved."

therefore

EGO DIES — CHRIST LIVES

(healthy self-image)

Refusal to accept/recognize this leads to

withdrawal
minimizes self-importance
feelings of inferiority
guilt
negative self-image

over-compensation
magnifies self-importance
feelings of superiority
pride
distorted self-image

SPIRITUAL DEFEAT

When You Minimize God's Opinion Of You

Until you come to grips with the fact that God completely accepts you because of what Christ did, you will never fully accept yourself. If you refuse to believe or accept the fact that God has received you, your self-image will be affected. When you minimize your importance in His eyes:

1. You depreciate your worth before God. The Apostle Paul wrote to the Romans, "For by the grace given me I say to every one of you: Do not think of yourself more highly than you ought..." (Romans 12:3a). And as we have already seen, if it is wrong to have too high an opinion of yourself, it is just as wrong to have too low an opinion of yourself.

One of the most thrilling things Jesus does is take somebody who seems to be nothing and then add Himself, giving that person infinite value and worth. When you suffer from feelings of worthlessness, remember that even when you take nothing and add Jesus to it, you don't end up with nothing. You end up with a vessel of clay filled with the very presence and power of God.

Take an old clay pot, virtually worthless, and put $1,000,000 worth of gold inside it. What is the intrinsic worth of what you have? Obviously, $1,000,000. In the same way, when Christ adds Himself to the most insignificant individual, that is a person of great value, redeemed by the very blood of Jesus Christ.

Actually, when you come to the place where you realize that you are nothing on your own, and you let God begin to work through you, it is amazing what can happen. Look at Moses. For the first forty years of his life, he was quite certain that he really was somebody. After all, he had been educated in the University of Egypt as the son of a Pharaoh. Nothing was spared to prepare him for a brilliant future.

One day Moses saw an Egyptian harassing an Israelite and decided to help God out by sinking his dagger into the man's back. He would settle the score; and as the blood ran down into the desert sand, Moses became a murderer. For the next forty years, he ran as a fugitive from Egyptian justice. He realized that instead of being a somebody, he was a nobody—a zero with the circle rubbed out. That was when God appeared to him one day, speaking to him from a burning bush.

Had Moses ever changed! When God said, "Moses, I want you to go to Pharaoh and deliver my people." Moses said, "Not me, Lord! I'm just not the man to handle the job. I've been out here in the desert as a sheepherder for the past forty years." Then Moses found out what God can do with somebody who realizes he is nobody. For the next forty years, he was God's chosen leader of Israel.

2. A negative self-image results. Symptoms of a negative self-image are self-pity, depression, inadequacy, and feelings of worthlessness and inferiority. You become extremely critical of yourself and begin to withdraw from people. You are sure that you can't perform as well as others, and you tend not to try. You see yourself as very plain or just homely. You think that you aren't intelligent enough to move up the ladder of promotion—and in time your conduct matches the negative image in your thinking.

I have known men and women who have gone through life defeated and downcast because they considered themselves to be of no real value. Some have been graduates of Christian universities who refused to teach a Sunday School class or even usher in a church service because of hang-ups over the past.

There are times when families contribute to this problem rather than help to alleviate it. Take, for instance, the young woman who wrote the following:

"I am twenty-seven years old. This is hard to admit, but I need help. I was conceived out-of-wedlock which forced my mother into an early marriage at the age of 16. I definitely was not wanted and have always known it because my home was violent. This has made me feel unwanted in all situations. After my brother died, I went through a suicidal crisis.... As a result, I was disfellowshipped from the church. My question is this. Can I come to God and have fellowship with Him? I did sin terribly in wanting to commit suicide, and I didn't come into the world in God's perfect will so I find it very difficult to believe. Please answer my letter because I am hurting on the inside."

Who wouldn't hurt having grown up with a home situation like this? When you struggle with feelings of inferiority, ask yourself, "Are these feelings from God?" Of course, your answer should be in the negative. C. S. Lewis, the Oxford University professor, once wrote that you sometimes have to tell your feelings *where to get off.* Feeling inferior is such a time. Regardless of your feelings, you must remind yourself that you are a person of value in God's sight. No one can make you feel inferior unless you allow him to do so.

3. You are buffeted by unmerited guilt. Another characteristic of the individual who minimizes the importance of self is constant harassment by guilt feelings. Sarah was like that. I met Sarah for the first time when I was asked to visit her two-month-old girl, born with five tiny holes in her heart. Doctors told the parents that the tiny holes would enlarge as the baby grew older and that nothing could be done. Life expectancy was about two years, and that would be punctuated by suffering and constant medical attention.

At Children's Hospital, I donned a white gown and mask to enter the room where the little baby lay. As I stood up by the side of the crib and looked down into the face of that innocent little girl, the mother turned to me and with tears in her eyes blurted out, "Why is God punishing my baby for what I have done?"

As we walked the hospital corridor together, Sarah told me how she had grown up in a home with little love. Her parents were strict disciplinarians who would tell her, "God will get you if you are bad." Her concept of God was that of a cosmic policeman in hobnailed boots who will grind you into the asphalt when you are bad.

At the age of sixteen, Sarah decided to have her fun, no matter what God did to her. For a period of time she lived a rather careless life. Then, a couple of years later as she walked down the street, she heard music drifting out of the open windows of a church. She hesitated, then slipped into the building where she heard a simple message of God's love and forgiveness. She went forward and prayed to receive Christ as her personal Savior, although not understanding the nature of God's forgiveness.

After she married, a series of disasters befell the young couple. Each time something happened, Sarah was certain that God was punishing her for what she did before she became a Christian. A flood devastated their little home, completely destroying all their possessions. The couple's first child was stillborn, and now this little baby had been born with five tiny holes in her heart.

Was God punishing Sarah's child for what Sarah had done? No, of course not! "Therefore, if anyone is in Christ, he is a new creation; the old has gone, the new has come" (2 Corinthians 5:17). But Sarah didn't realize that. The continued guilt that she felt was just as real as though God had directly been delivering His vengeance on her family.

That night I prayed, "Oh, God, please let this child live so that this mother will know when You forgive us, You wipe the slate clean as though we had never sinned." Over time, Sarah accepted the fact that God had forgiven her, and that the problem with her child wasn't punishment for the sins of her past. Christ had long since forgiven them.

That child, not expected to live beyond the age of two, was a very normal, healthy teenager at my last contact: the five tiny holes in her heart knit together—nothing short of a miracle!

What else happens when you cannot accept yourself as a person of value and worth in the sight of God?

4. Personal appearance often becomes neglected. A negative self-image can cause you to reason, "Since I'm not any good anyway, why should I be concerned about my weight or how I look?" Soon, you have neglected yourself and are carrying around an extra thirty pounds of not-so-beautiful weight. You don't bother to keep your hair and nails groomed properly. You expect to be inferior because you think you are. When you suffer from feelings of negative self-image, you can allow yourself to rapidly become what you fear you are already.

When you realize what worth you have in the sight of God, it is easier to realize that your body is the literal dwelling place of God, the Holy Spirit. "Do you not know that your body is a temple of the Holy Spirit, who is in you...?" wrote Paul to the Corinthians. "You are not your own; you have been bought at a price" (1 Corinthians 6:19, 20). Acknowledging that the price was paid at Calvary gives incentive to make yourself the person of value and worth which you really are.

In this section, I've discussed characteristics of a negative self-image, someone who suffers from a sense of inferiority. Now, let's take a look at the characteristics of the person who tries to overcompensate for perceived short-comings because he hasn't found the liberating truth that he can simply be himself.

When You Overcompensate

1. You have an inflated opinion of your own self-worth. When you really understand that God will accept you on the basis of what Christ did, you don't have to prove to the world how great you are. You can take a deep breath and just be yourself, which is a great feeling! You don't have to be a put-on or a sham. Someone has said that ego *is edging God out.* But when Christ lives in you, ego is pushed aside. This allows you to be genuine, authentic, and real!

But the man or woman suffering from a lack of self-acceptance doesn't know that freedom. He or she has to let you know how important he or she really is. This person usually considers himself or herself to be indispensable. The fact is that this person is very expendable. Friends might tend to humor the person or disregard the grandiose, "How-great-I-am" statements. Actually, however, life might go on pretty much the same whether or not that person is present, and things might even sometimes run a good deal smoother when that person is absent.

2. Status is very important. When you struggle with your identity because you do not realize God accepts you as you are, you want people to know that you have taken your place in society. You tend to flash your jewels or assets in such a way that people can't help noticing. Your image and status are very important. You want to be served, not serve others. You want people to know that you have an important pedigree, have been to the right schools (if they can't see that large class ring, you'll tell them anyway!), and have a very prestigious circle of friends.

The kind of a car you drive, the labels in your clothes, and even the brand of watch you wear has to convey the message: "I'm better than you!" or, at least, "I'm very, very good!"

I think of a young man who was driving down the interstate. A truck got too close to him, sideswiping his new sports

42

car. When the vehicles stopped, the man was moaning, "Look at what you did to the side of my BMW!"

"Forget your BMW," said the truck driver. "Look at your arm. It's mangled!" Immediately, the young man looked down and moaned, "My Rolex watch is gone, too!"

Do you have talents? Then, remember that God is the one who gave you the ability to do what you are able to accomplish. On the walls of the sound stage of Unusual Films is a sign that reads, "Every good gift and every perfect gift comes down from the Father above...so why should you boast?"

Do you have money? Then, remember that the Scripture says, "It is he who is gives you the ability to produce wealth" (Deuteronomy 8:18). Don't forget that what you have today can be wiped out overnight with a bad business decision. If the market falls, the stock you own can be worth half as much six months from now. What you have been given by your Heavenly Father is yours to use, not abuse. You don't own it; it has well been said that hearses never have U-Haul trailers attached to them. Your wealth is a loan, a stewardship which God has entrusted to you.

People who are secure, who know who they are, don't find it necessary to let you know how much money they have, or who their best friends are, or what things cost. It's not important to them.

Do you have prestige and influence? Then, remember that promotion comes from neither the east or the west, but it is God who raises one up and sets another aside (Psalm 75: 6,7). God denounces pride as a vicious sin. Proverbs 6:16-18 lists several things that God hates. One of those is *haughty eyes*. And we have all heard the wisdom of Proverbs 16:18: "Pride goes before destruction, a haughty spirit before a fall."

3. You are quick to recognize flaws in others, slow to see them in yourself. Frankly, it doesn't take a lot of talent to look

at another person and see what's wrong with that person. It is a totally different matter, however, to look at yourself and see your own weaknesses.

4. You want to be known by your association with others. Belonging to the right club or the right church, having the right friends, or being *in* is very important. These individuals usually drop names unnecessarily in conversation. For example someone might say, "Yesterday, I was with Bill Yates, the president of Microhard, the corporation that has made so much money on their new software, and he was telling me about...." A person like this might tend to let others know the cost of his vacation, or what he paid for his clothes or computer.

At the opposite end of the same spectrum is the individual who feels he or she has to let you know that the new dress was on sale, or that he got his suit at the thrift store. Either way, he is identifying with a way of doing things—either paying the most or getting the biggest bargain.

Acceptance In A Biblical Perspective

We've already said that, in the context of Christian faith, my self-acceptance should be based on the fact that God will freely accept me because of what Christ has done. Therefore, I don't have to constantly fight feelings of inferiority and inadequacy, which produce guilt and a troubled conscience. Neither do I have to constantly try to prove to myself and to others how good I really am. I don't need to base my self-acceptance on material possessions or physical attributes, thinking that others will accept me for what I have or possess.

That God should have a personal interest in each of us as individuals is a tremendous thought! Here is the great big universe—so large that it defies human comprehension. Yet, in the midst of it, God is interested in me as an individual person.

And He doesn't stop there. God gives to each of us who knows Christ certain spiritual gifts to enrich our lives and the lives of others. Paul wrote to the Corinthians that the outworking of the Holy Spirit is given to each believer for his profit (1 Corinthians 12:7), whatever that outworking might be. Then, Paul enumerates the gifts, saying that God has given each of us certain gifts that equip us for His work. Never underestimate the scope of your influence. God gave you the gifts you have, and He has a purpose for them and for you.

Your life touches a circle of friends. No matter how limited you think your influence is, for good or evil, nobody else can influence lives in quite the same way you can.

A little lady who lived by herself once said, "Oh, I never get out, so there is no one whose life I can influence for the Lord." A friend challenged her to keep a list of the people who came to her front door, and to pray for each of them. First, the postman came with a delivery; then a boy came to collect for the newspaper. Later, a neighbor stopped by to talk about a community drive. Little by little, the list began to grow. This person, called a "shut-in," realized that she still touched lives that were, perhaps, overlooked by others.

What else does self-acceptance mean to a Christian? It means that God is at work in my life. *"Please be patient with me. God isn't finished with me yet!"* became a popular phrase some years back. We need to keep the truth of that in mind.

Two words can make all the difference in our perspective. Those words are because and becoming. When you use the word because, you blame God. "I am this way because…" mirrors hostility. When you realize that God is at work in your life, using circumstances to mold and shape your character, you begin to realize that you are in the process of becoming the person He wants you to be. You have a hope and a future.

What the Bible calls sanctification is really part of the Holy Spirit's ministry in our lives. God chips away at the rough edges of our lives and personalities, and he brings us into conformity with His will and purpose.

When you can accept yourself as a person of worth and value, it is easier to accept circumstances in life that are adverse. It is easier to remember that God has not forsaken you and He is not punishing you. Rather, He is still guiding the affairs of your life no matter what happens. You gain the assurance that you are not adrift on the ocean of life without a chart or compass.

What do you do when your baby is rushed to the hospital with a high fever and an infection that is consuming her energy and very life? You can wring your hands and cry, "Why my baby? Why are you picking on me, God?" Or you can fall back on the assurance that you belong to Him. Since you are adopted into His family, you can run to your Heavenly Father and cry out, "Lord, I really need your help right now!"

Self-acceptance, seen from a biblical perspective, produces strength in life's storms. You don't see life's difficulties as punishment because you already know that your sins have been dealt with and you are God's child. God does discipline His children in love (see Hebrews 12:3- 15), but keeping a biblical perspective helps you remember that God "works out everything in conformity with the purpose of his will" (Ephesians 1:11).

Self-acceptance in the context of Christian faith results in an inner radiance that comes from the indwelling presence of Christ in a life. An inner tranquillity and peace, a certain measure of security, results from being in touch with the Divine and knowing that He is fully in control of life's circumstances. We are to focus on the beauty that results from His presence in us rather than simply to be concerned with appearance (1 Peter 3:3-6).

A third thing self-acceptance does in a Christian context is produce a different value system, one that puts emphasis on character, integrity and spiritual values. Some people spend a large sum of money for a particular automobile when a smaller one would be satisfactory. Then, they might say something like, "I can't afford to give to God's work." When you make choices like that, you might really be saying, "My value system puts a much higher premium on a large car than on giving to God's work."

When you say, "I have no time to spend with my family," you might really mean, "Making money in the business is more important than my wife and children." "I don't have time to go to church," can be another way of saying, "I consider a day of leisure more important than worshipping God."

From God's point of view, a regenerated value system is a reflection of security and self-acceptance. A Christian perspective is that life is a cooperation of the human and the divine: "For we are God's workmanship, created in Christ Jesus to do good works" (Ephesians 2:10). Self-acceptance and a joyous, radiant life go hand-in-hand together. They aren't synonymous but they complement each other.

Who are you? Understanding that He has already received us enables us to receive ourselves so that we may boldly say:

"I'm a person of great value and worth."

"I'm a person whom Jesus loves, so I can love myself."

"I'm a person who is becoming the person God wants me to be."

"I'm just me and I wouldn't want to be anybody else in all the world!"

When you feel your self-image slipping and you begin to forget who you are, lift your head and look up; it's important to know you are the child of a King and be proud of it. This is one of the ways we win our inner struggles and become all that God intends us to be.

Discussion Questions:

John grew up in a broken home; his father left when John was two years old. Since he was the fifth child, he wore hand-me-down clothes and he had to fight for attention. He later put himself through college by waiting tables at two restaurants. Now, as an adult, he constantly puts other people down, brags about his influential contacts, and refuses to listen to criticism at work.

1. John seems very confident of himself and his life. How might his behavior be seen as a *cover up* for feelings of insecurity?

2. What is one area in your life that you used to either minimize or overcompensate for that you no longer do? How did that change happen?

3. Appearance, performance and influence are three things that people use to try to impress others. What is one thing in each of these categories that you are sometimes tempted to use to impress others? How is that connected to areas of insecurity, and what steps can you take to stop your pattern of overcompensating?

4. Name one thing that you do not like about yourself. As you see it, what is one way that this characteristic has a negative affect on your life? Name three ways that this can be a positive thing for you. If you have trouble seeing it as a positive thing, think about someone you know who has the same *defect,* whether to the same degree as you or not, who does not seem troubled by that characteristic. What are three ways that person might say the characteristic positively impacts his life?

This will hurt....

When you feel like you have something to prove, whether to yourself or to other people, it will hurt to react automatically, following the course of habit. It will hurt to belittle another person or step in to show how much more competent you are.

This will help....

Learn to identify that puffed-up feeling for what it is—an insecurity. Look for ways you can redirect your thinking. Ask a trusted friend to help you begin to see those things as insecurities.

It will help to take a look at people you know who are very secure. Cultivate the qualities you see in them in your own life.

CHAPTER THREE

Making Your Emotions Work For You

"Why did you do that?" Most of us have had the experience of asking someone that question. Parents, especially, can relate to that! And the response most often is, "Oh, I just felt like it."

The feelings that stem from our emotions are powerful forces. But are we subject to their whims and fancies, driven by their great powers to and fro in life, powerless against them? Are our emotions subject to our wills or our wills subject to our emotions?" Let's look further at the powerful force of our emotions and the great inner struggles that they create.

"Emotions," says Drever's Dictionary of Psychology, "are a state of excitement or perturbation, marked by strong feelings and usually an impulse towards a definite form of behavior."[1] The Miriam-Webster dictionary puts it like this: "...a departure from the normal calm state to strong feelings, an impulse towards action." Some of you who have struggled through a few years of Latin in school may remember that our English word emotion comes from the Latin participle emotum meaning "to move."

Emotions are to life what pigment is to paint: they make life bright and beautiful, or dark and dreary. Someone once hit the nail on the head when he said, "Man is not a rational creature with emotions; rather, he is an emotional creature who is rational." Regardless of how you describe them, emotions are the prime movers of life.

Emotions Add Color To Life's Landscape

What would music, art, poetry, or literature be without emotions? Remove emotions from these great disciplines and from others like them, and life would become sterile and barren; the landscape of living would become desolate and cold.

Ignace Paderewski, a great Polish pianist and, incidentally, the first president of Poland, was a person of great emotional sensitivity. When the great maestro was scheduled to play a concert in a building, he would go to that place several hours before the concert began, and sit quietly soaking up the ambiance of the facility so that the room became a part of him. Once the concert began, nothing about the building would distract him or inhibit the flow of music that came from his innermost being.

Fritz Kreisler, a great violinist, once made arrangements to meet a friend when his train stopped at a certain town en route to a concert. Kreisler tucked his precious violin under his arm and eagerly disembarked to find his friend. When it came time to board the train again, Kreisler began searching for his ticket. To his chagrin, it was nowhere to be found. He tried to convince the ticket collector that he really was Fritz Kreisler and that he left his ticket on the train.

The skeptical agent eyed the violin under his arm. "If you really are Fritz Kreisler," he said, "then let me hear you play your violin, because nobody in the world can play like Fritz Kreisler." There on the train platform, Kreisler opened his well-worn violin case and played for the skeptical but pleased ticket agent.

What was it that made Kreisler's playing so distinct that even an amateur musician would know the difference? His brilliant emotional sensitivity!

Emotions Are The Prime Movers Of People

What impact would the words of Winston Churchill during World War 2 have had if they had not been impregnated with emotion? This great orator inspired and moved the very soul of the British people during the difficult war years. When the bombs fell and a German invasion seemed imminent, Churchill's words marshaled reserves of steel as he said, "A thousand years from now all the world will say this was Britain's finest hour!"

Across the cold English Channel the mad Fuhrer also moved people with emotions. His fiery rhetoric inspired the cheering masses who quickly became mesmerized by his forceful words.

No orator, artist, minister, writer or poet has ever succeeded in his profession without the ability to use emotion in such a way that the lives of people are deeply touched.

The Welsh revival near the turn of the century shook that little country for God. It was triggered by the words of a teenage girl who stood up in a mid-week prayer meeting: "I do love Jesus...." Then she began sobbing as she repeated the words. Unable to maintain her composure, she sat down and continued to weep softly. The deeply stirred feelings of her heart, fed by the fervent prayers of God's people, began to spread, and revival broke out.

A study of the life of Christ shows that He was a man of emotional sensitivity and deep feeling. Consider these words: "When Jesus landed and saw a large crowd, he had compassion on them and healed their sick" (Matthew 14:14). Jesus wept at the tomb of His friend, Lazarus. He cried over His beloved Jerusalem, saying, "O Jerusalem, Jerusalem, you who kill the prophets and stone those sent to you, how often I have longed to gather your children together, as a hen gathers her chicks under her wings, but you were not willing" (Luke 13:34).

Although there is no record of Jesus' ever being moved to laughter, I am convinced that He did laugh, not with a garrulous emptiness that produces the ribald laughter of many today—but with a sense of humor which originated deep within His heart.

Jesus empathized with people in their deepest needs, showing us that the display of emotions is not a sign of weakness. Emotions manifest what is in your heart. This is what makes you human instead of a robot that moves on command or impulse to do the bidding of a controlling power.

Three Principle Emotions—Love, Anger, Fear

Psychologist John B. Watson contends that we are born with three principal emotions—love, anger, and fear. From these three basic emotions come a plethora of other emotions: disgust, shame, tenderness, awe, reverence, joy, grief, jealousy, pride, greed, hatred, ecstasy, remorse, excitement, envy, worry, and happiness.[2]

There are times when more than one emotion sways you. Sometimes emotions that seem to be opposites—love and hatred, for example—are both present. Ambivalence, as psychologists describe it, occurs when you feel two opposing emotions at the same time, each pulling you a different way.

It is perfectly normal to feel opposing emotions with people you really care about. You'll feel that way when you discover your four-year-old has written, "I LOVE YOU, MOMMY!" on the wall with your lipstick. You'll feel that way when your youngster brings in a bouquet of flowers for you which he picked...from your neighbor's garden.

A newspaper article told of a man whose tiny boat overturned in the South China sea. He later told reporters that he was happy, but fearful—happy because it was the first time in two months that his wife clung to him, but fearful because he couldn't swim and the waters were full of sharks.

The Bible And Your Emotions

What does the Bible say about emotions and how we handle them? Does God view some emotions as good and other emotions as harmful? Or, has He pretty well left us on our own at this point?

Emotions so have an impact on your emotional, physical and spiritual well-being. The writers of Scripture saw three emotions as generally negative or detrimental, and three others as generally positive or contributing to your overall health and happiness. The *negative* emotions are fear, hatred, and anger; the *positive* emotions are faith, love, and peace.

These six emotions stand in sharp contrast to each other:

Potentially Positive	Potentially Negative
Fear	Faith
Hatred	Love
Anger	Peace

This principle doesn't hold up as a hard and fast rule, but it is generally recognized that anger, hatred, and fear have greater negative potential while faith, love, and peace have greater positive potential. However, the three emotions that I categorize as potentially negative can also be positive and are not always wrong from a Christian perspective. There is a place for all emotions in life. Even negative emotions, properly used, become constructive. Still, faith, love, and peace, by their very nature, have a greater tendency to produce results in life that are beneficial to your physical and emotional well-being.

Emotions And Your Physical body

All competent medical authorities are quick to recognize the relationship between your emotions and your physical well-being. In his book, *None of These Diseases,* Dr. S. I. McMillen asks the question, "Is it not a remarkable fact that our reactions to stress determine whether stress is going to cure us or make us sick?"[3] Your attitude determines whether emotions will make you *better* or *bitter.*

Positive emotions add vitality to life. The way you view the circumstances of your life, whether negatively or positively, may make the difference between life and death in extremely difficult situations. This fact was shown by the experiences of prisoners of war in the concentration camps of Europe in World War 2.

Viktor Frankl was one of those prisoners who lived to tell about it. In his book, *Man's Search for Meaning*, Frankl describes how those who gave up hope often curled up in fetal positions and died while those who were committed to strong religious beliefs somehow survived. He writes,

> "The prisoner who had lost faith in the future—his future—was doomed. With his loss of belief in the future, he also lost his spiritual hold; he let himself decline and became subject to mental and physical decay.... He simply gave up. There he remained... nothing bothered him any more."[4]

When you are confronted with danger, your emotions trigger your adrenaline system, and it pumps large doses of this powerful substance into your blood stream. This enables you to perform almost superhuman feats. No doubt you have read or heard of situations where this is true. Say a car has overturned and someone is trapped underneath. In this life or death situation, people have been known to single-handedly lift the automobile to free the person trapped under it.

When my son was about two years old, we lived in a suburban area fairly close to the woods. Reports of wild dog packs attacking children caused us to exercise as much caution as possible, but no parent can keep a two-year-old confined to the house all the time. I was in the study when suddenly I heard loud barking and the frantic screams of a child—my only son, Steven.

The instant the sound registered in my brain, I leaped for the door. My only thought was to rescue Steven. I did not notice that the screen door was firmly latched, and I sailed through it, knocking the latch off as though it was not there. As soon as the stray German shepherd saw me, the dog turned and ran. That probably saved its life—I am certain I would have killed that dog with my bare hands, regardless of how badly mauled I might have been in the process.

At the time, I felt nothing as I crashed through the door, but in the days that followed my left side turned black and blue from the impact. That's the force of adrenaline triggered by an emotional response.

Negative emotions can literally destroy you physically. Emotions affect a variety of physical systems—the number of red corpuscles, the reduction of conscious fatigue under stress, the rate of your heart beat, respiration, and even your temperature.

Bitterness, hatred, envy, anger, and other negative feelings trigger harmful responses to our physical bodies. Helen Kooiman tells of a well-known doctor of internal medicine at Mayo Clinic who used to say, "I tell my patients they cannot afford grudges or maintain hate." The doctor went on to give an illustration of how he saw a man kill himself, as he put it, "inch-by-inch," because of a quarrel with a sister over a family estate. The man became so embittered within himself that his breath was foul, and the organs of his body ceased to function properly, and in a matter of months he was physically dead."[5] The man literally killed himself a day at a time.

Negative emotions are the root causes of psychosomatic illnesses. The fact that something is labeled as *psychosomatic* doesn't, for a moment, mean that the illness is not real. It is very real. What this means is that the physical problem—be it an ulcer, hypertension, heart trouble, or a skin rash—is triggered by an emotional response.

Psychologists believe that 60 percent of all hospital beds are filled with patients whose problems are psychosomatic in origin. Some, as Dr. Dennis Cope, believe the figure is much higher. Cope, voted outstanding professor at the UCLA School of Medicine in Los Angeles, is an endocrinologist, a committed believer in Jesus Christ, and active in his church. I asked him if he believed that the percentage is that high. He thought for a moment. "Actually," he said, "I believe the figure runs much closer to 80 or 85 percent!" What a price to pay for negative emotions!

Consider the following:

- A study of 5000 gastro-intestinal disorders at Oschner Clinic in New Orleans concluded that 74 percent of the problems were emotionally induced.

- The out-patient clinic of New York University has stated that 76 percent of their patients are there because of emotional stress.

- A study at the University of Colorado's Department of Medicine indicated that the majority of their patients harbored deep-seated bitterness, grudges against someone, or resentment over something.

- A study conducted by John Schindler, M.D., claims that emotions tighten the skeletal and muscular internal organs and lead to emotional arthritis—Schindler's study is available in most medical libraries.

The Bible says negative emotions are to be dealt with immediately, that bitterness is to be expunged from the heart. When conflict exists between individuals, the conflict should be promptly resolved (see Matthew 18:15). McMillen is right—emotions will make you either better or bitter. They will either kill or cure. They will be either a cause for rejoicing or a curse.

Emotions And Your Mind

Your emotions are not rigid like pieces of steel cast in concrete. They are fluid and flexible, extremely complex. They bend with your physical feelings and the impulses of mental conditioning that affect your thinking. The Bible tell us that as a man thinks in his heart, so is he (See Proverbs 23:7, KJV). Your thinking is what gives guidance to your emotions, either negatively or positively. Either it contributes to the inner struggles you have, or it lessens them.

Emotions can be conditioned. Most introductory psychology courses review the experiments by Ivan Pavlov, demonstrating the fact that emotional responses follow the conditioning to which they have been subjected. Let me illustrate.

Suppose you are standing on a street corner watching a parade. It is a big event, and units have come from many different countries to participate. The different units march past you, each bearing the flag of its home country. You watch, perhaps politely clapping your hands in acknowledgment. Then, the color guard of your own country marches by. The sight of your flag deeply stirs the feelings of your heart. You can't help it—you choke up and a tear comes to your eye.

Why? The flag of your country is simply a piece of cloth of various colors stitched onto a background—just like the other flags that preceded it. The difference is that everything you love is wrapped up in what it represents—your home, your country, and your people. It represents what you live for. The sight of the flag waving in the breeze triggers the emotional response of your heart.

Our emotions can also be conditioned in such a way that what we once felt strongly just doesn't exist anymore. In psychological warfare, we call it brainwashing. A person's psychological resistance is so battered that he gradually begins to believe and think what he otherwise would have rejected.

When it comes to our lives and marriages, the same thing— though perhaps in a slightly different manner—is true. Strong emotions such as love and faith can be battered by circumstances that gradually cause those strong feelings to subside or even to die.

Emotions are flexible and can be channeled into productive areas. It is important that your emotions be subject to your will. First, accountability before God demands it. Man is a responsible individual capable of controlling his behavior, regardless of what he feels (see Deuteronomy 24:16; Ezekiel 18:19-23; Romans 3:23).

Let's go one step further. God created man as an emotional being and He holds man accountable. If an individual was not capable of keeping himself from doing what he feels pulled to do by his emotions, and yet God still held him accountable for his actions, then God would be an unfair judge.

When there is a struggle between the emotions and the will, the emotions win out only when you disregard the power of your own will. When you choose to let emotions control your behavior, you have, as an act of your will, decided to bypass your intellect.

"But, I love him; I can't help it!"

"I just don't feel like praying so I won't be a hypocrite doing something I don't feel like doing!"

"Surely it can't be wrong, because God gave me those beautiful feelings and I was doing what came naturally!"

Statements like these reflect the popular notion that people are not really responsible when they act on the emotional responses of the human body. What about you—are you subject to the whims and fancies or your emotions?

Either your thinking will control your emotions or your emotions will control your thinking. The Bible says a great deal about your thinking and its relationship to your emotions. Consider these statements:

"Commit thy works unto the LORD and thy thoughts shall be established" (Proverbs 16:3, KJV).

"We demolish arguments and every pretension that sets itself up against the knowledge of God, and we take captive every thought to make it obedient to Christ" (2 Corinthians 10:5).

Negative thinking can be redirected.

The Bible also instructs us to focus on positive thoughts, which in turn bring wholesome emotional responses. "Finally, brothers," wrote Paul, "whatever is true, whatever is noble, whatever is right, whatever is pure, whatever is lovely…think about such things" (Philippians. 4:8).

You will never be able to fully control your environment. There will always be people who rub you the wrong way, the weather won't always suit you, and neighbors may not please you. But you will never be in a position where you cannot choose your emotional response to your environment. This knowledge is liberating.

Viktor Frankl believed that people who were imprisoned in the concentration camps of World War 2 made a fundamental decision as to whether they would act or react to their circumstances, and their decision had everything to do with their destiny.

In the final analysis it becomes clear that the sort of person the prisoner became was the result of an inner decision, and not the result of camp influences alone. Fundamentally, therefore, any man can, even under such circumstances, decide what shall become of him…. He may retain his human dignity even in a concentration camp.[6]

In the final analysis nobody forces you to be controlled by your environment, your poverty, or the conditions of your childhood. You have a choice. You decide how you will act, whether you return evil with evil, or evil with good. Nobody can keep you from loving a person no matter how unlovable he is, and no one can keep you from hating him if you allow yourself to do so. The choice is yours.

A businessman who bought a newspaper from a lad on the street every evening as he left his office learned that lesson. When he took the paper, the man would always say, "Thank you, son. Thanks very much!" One day the boy asked, "How come you always say 'Thank you!'? Other people don't bother."

"I was once a newsboy myself," replied the business man. "I know what it is to be considered as nothing, and I determined never to treat anybody like that!"

Making Emotions Work For You

Because your emotions follow the nod of your intellect, there is a very definite sense in which you do direct your emotional responses. It is how you do it that makes the difference. There are three ways emotions can be handled.

1. Emotions can be repressed. To constantly repress your emotions by bottling them up inside is harmful emotionally, physically, and spiritually. In a sense, expressing deep emotions works like a relief valve; it keeps stress and pressure from building up to the point where you explode. The longer you repress your emotions, especially negative emotions, the more volcanic their display will be when they finally come boiling to the surface. But because some people have grown up with the attitude that emotional display is weakness—men in particular are supposed to be tough and not cry—it is difficult to express emotions, and the

longer normal expression is denied the more devastating the consequences are.

A father lost a son who was in his early twenties. When the news of the boy's death reached the family, the boy's mother burst into tears. But the father turned ashen white, clenched his teeth, and fought back the tears. "John really took it like a man," his friends said. "Never shed a tear!"

They were right, too, until the funeral. The minister concluded his remarks, and the people silently filed past the casket as the organ played softly, "Nearer my God to Thee." Then, the boy's father said quietly, "God, I'll get even with You if it's the last thing I ever do." He paused. "God," he repeated, "I'll get even with You…" Suddenly, he realized what he was saying and the tears poured out. As A. W. Tozer wrote, "Be sure that human feelings can never be completely stifled. If they are forbidden their normal course, like a river they will cut another channel through the life and flow out to curse, and ruin, and destroy."[7]

The display of emotion, whether it is in times of grief or excitement, is not weakness. And repressing emotions, which are part of our psychic make-up, can even be a contributing factor to mental illness.

2. Emotions can be denied. This differs from repression in that the person who denies emotions refuses to admit that they exist, or to come to grips with issues that would provide emotional responses of any kind. But you can't ignore emotions indefinitely, just like you can't ignore a pair of shoes that is getting scuffed. Eventually, you have to notice the marks!

One gentleman, though, nearly succeeded. At the age of eighty, his doctor gave him a clean bill of health and pronounced him a nearly perfect specimen.

"What's the secret of your good health?" asked the doctor.

"It's this way, Doc," the old man said. "When Sarah and I married fifty-five years ago, we decided that we wouldn't allow ourselves to get angry with each other. I told her that instead of arguing with her, I'd just get my hat and take a long walk.... So, you see, Doc, I've had a vigorous outdoor life now for many years!"

Some folks try to sidestep emotional issues rather than meet them and resolve them. When they are confronted with situations that could be emotional, such as family problems, talking to a boss, or dividing an estate, they will live with those situations for years, even with deep-seated feelings, and ignore the problem. They both repress and deny their emotions.

Ignoring emotional feelings never contributes to the stability of a marriage or any relationship. Feelings that are repressed or ignored do not go away. They produce strong feelings of bitterness, and those feelings will eat at a person and have a negative impact.

A young soldier came to me for counseling. His wife had decided that she didn't love him, and she was not certain that she ever had. She was not in love with anyone else, and she had been true to him. However, ten years before that, he had confessed to her that, when he was overseas, he had had a sexual relationship with a girl who really didn't mean anything to him. It was during a time of loneliness and weakness. A nasty argument followed. Without resolving the issue, they had agreed "never to mention the incident again." There wasn't a day, however, when she didn't think of it. Until the situation was faced and resolved, the horrible turmoil that created stress on their marriage did not lessen.

Attempting to ignore your emotions by saying, "Let's just not talk about it," or "Well, it was your fault as much as it was mine, so let's just forget it," doesn't resolve the problem.

3. Emotions can be externalized in a positive way. Just *getting emotions out of your system* is not enough. Lucy, Charlie Brown's sidekick in the comic strip Peanuts, was angry with her little brother, Linus. Her fist was drawn back, ready to sock him. Linus backed into a corner and yelled, "Stop, Lucy! Let's talk about this! Nations are fighting each other! People are in conflict, but let's not fight!"

Lucy stopped for a moment! She was visibly impressed at the logic of Linus, but the next picture shows, "POW!" She socked Linus and then said, "I had to hit 'em; he was beginning to make sense."

You may feel better when you vent your emotions by cutting loose and pouring out vindictive oaths. But, like squeezing the trigger of a machine gun, the damage is done once you do it that way.

So how do you constructively get those emotions out of your system? The Bible teaches that you can externalize those emotions in a healthy way. First, I suggest you relieve those bottled-up emotions by talking about them with someone who cares about you. Many times, when I counsel with someone, I will simply listen for an entire hour. About all I contribute to the conversation is an occasional, "Yes! I understand," "I see," or something else just as profound. But, at the end of that hour, the person will often say, "You have helped me so much!" A person feels immensely better when he has the opportunity just to get something off his chest. This is one way a person can externalize his or her emotions in a healthy way.

One of the Bible's profound psychological insights is that it clearly recognizes the importance of externalizing your emotions in proper ways. Jesus told us that if you have something against someone, or have a conflict with someone, you are to go to that person and share your conflict on a one-to-one basis (Matthew 18:15). By doing this you neither repress your emotions nor deny them; you externalize them. You deal with them in a way that helps you find permanent relief. Though we often try to avoid confrontation, at times it's vitally necessary in facing issues that must be faced.

Another thing you can do is to bring your burden and emotional fatigue to God in prayer. There's a big difference between sharing your concern with someone else and sharing it with God. You will feel better if you share your emotions with a friend, but all a friend can do is listen. When you share them with God, He can touch your heart and relieve the stress and strain you feel. But He doesn't stop there. He can also touch the hearts of those for whom you pray, allowing His divine power to melt and mold hearts and lives to the configuration of His will.

The third stanza of the well-known hymn, "What a Friend We Have in Jesus," is especially meaningful to this discussion:

Are we weak and heavy laden,
    Cumbered with a load of care?
Precious Savior, still our refuge—
    Take it to the Lord in prayer.
Do thy friends despise, forsake thee?
    Take it to the Lord in prayer;
In His arms He'll take and shield thee—
    Thou wilt find a solace there.

The words of Joseph Scriven's hymn come from a painful experience he endured. The Canadian school teacher was engaged to be married when an untimely accident took the life of the one he so loved. Unquestionably, Scriven wrote of the hiding place that he had found in the friendship of a Savior who loved him, and who understood the pent-up emotions that he couldn't express to others.

Jesus has faced the gamut of life's emotions from birth to death. He knows how you feel when you find it so difficult to share even with a husband or a wife. He knows and He understands. When you pray, open your heart and let the feelings flow out. Are you angry? Do you think God doesn't know it? Then, tell Him in no uncertain terms.

Is your heart filled with hatred toward someone? Then let it flow out in prayer. You will discover that God alone can turn your hatred to love by the alchemy of grace and faith.

Is your heart filled with fear that immobilizes you and renders you inactive? Then, let God speak to your heart: "And surely I am with you always, to the very end of the age (Matthew 28:20)."

Down through the centuries wise men have found a rest and a solace in prayer. Picture Abraham as he took his son to Mount Moriah and prayed. Picture Moses, the great leader of God's people, in intercession for Israel. If you can, picture our Lord agonizing in the Garden of Gethsemane when He sweat great drops of blood. What emotion! What courage born in prayer!

Emotions can be warm and beautiful. Too many people's lives are gray because they are dominated by negative emotions instead of letting positive emotions be the pigment that enriches the landscape of their lives.

But can people change? Can life be different for those who are overwhelmed by negative emotions? Can they learn to let positive ones replace the negative ones in their lives? That's the focus of the next chapter. It's all part of winning your inner struggles.

Discussion Questions:

Bob's dad always told him, "Real men don't cry; now choke up those tears." Eventually, he learned how. Now that he's married, he finds it extremely difficult to show any emotion at all. His wife, Mary, desperately needs for him to show some tenderness toward her. He says he wants to, but he just can't seem to do it.

1. What is one thing Bob could do to start learning how to express his emotions rather than to repress them?

2. Take a look at your life. Name one sinful fear, one hatred, and one sinful anger. How can faith help you deal with that fear? How can love help you deal with that hatred? How can peace help you deal with that anger?

3. Which are you more likely to do—repress, deny or externalize your emotions in a productive way? What are some steps you can take or are taking in a healthy direction?

This will hurt....

Stereotypes are not easily overcome. It is our cultural tendency for men to repress or deny emotions in deference to their will; it is the tendency for women to *feel* their way through situations. It will hurt if you continue to make excuses for yourself or others because *men and women were created that way.*

The two extremes we usually face are either to be tossed about on the waves of our emotions, or to be in dry dock. It will hurt to tip the balance in either direction.

This will help....

A person becomes very vulnerable when he expresses his emotions. In order to create a *safe place* for someone who is learning to express emotions, you must keep his confidence. Remember that the other person owns his emotions, and sharing them with you does not give you permission to pass them out to whomever you choose.

Learning to make *I feel* statements instead of *you* statements will help in two ways. First, it will help keep communication between two people clear. Rather than accusing, "When you do that, you make me feel...," say, "I feel when that happens." *I feel* statements also help you to identify what it is you are feeling instead of focusing on what the other person is doing.

Notes

[1]Drever's Dictionary of Psychology as quoted by A. W. Tozer in *That Incredible Christian* (Harrisburg, Pennsylvania, Christian Publications, Inc., 1964), p. 49.

[2]Tozer, Ibid.

[3]S. I. McMillen, *None of These Diseases* (Old Tappan, N.J.: Flemming H. Revell Company), 1964 edition, p. 15.

[4]Viktor Frankl, *Man's Search for Meaning,* (New York: Washington Square Press, 1968), pp. 213, 214.

[5]Helen Kooiman, *Forgiveness in Action,* p. 19

[6]A. W. Tozer, Ibid. p. 49.

[7]Frankl, Ibid.

CHAPTER FOUR

Memories That Cause Inner Struggles

The human brain is an amazing phenomenon. It consists of 10 billion nerve units known as neurons. They are surrounded by a mass, 90 percent by bulk, of a jelly-like substance known as neuroglia—from the Greek word for glue, glia. The average adult human brain weighs about three pounds, and it's divided into three hemispheres. One of the hemispheres is known as the temporal lobe, and it concerns itself with your emotions and memory. Even with all the knowledge that science has acquired about the human brain, there is still much that is unknown. One thing we do know is that, though the human brain processes more than 10,000 thoughts every day, only a scant 3 percent of it is actually utilized. Though scientists say that the human brain is far superior to any computer ever invented, it is unfair to suggest a comparison to a computer. No computer, regardless of its sophistication, can rival the human brain with its vast scope of emotions and comprehension.

There is, however, a function of computers that I sometimes wish the human brain had: I wish we could input a command that would erase or delete certain events that have been indelibly written in the memory.

Shock therapy, used a lot in the 1950's and early 1960's, was an attempt to electrically remove certain events or memories from the brain that cause grief and pain.

But God has a better way—the healing of the emotions.

Memories That Scar Our Lives Are Commonplace

From a seventy-year-old woman came the following letter:

I was so interested in what you said about memories and how they can ruin the joy that we should have in our Christian walk. I am seventy-years-old and have lived a full and eventful life and have as you might probably know, memories that both bless and burn, a few that hurt deeply, and you helped me to feel I might be able to get rid of the ones that have burned so deeply.

Memories that burn, as she described them, are the ones that come back to haunt us. They rob us of our peace of mind and they create those inner struggles that haunt some people for an entire lifetime. That was true of a pastor friend of mine whose wife faced the prospect of either having surgery or spending the rest of her life invalid in a wheel chair. The two of them talked and prayed, sought counsel, and weighed the odds in their minds. They tried to visualize how they would cope with life if she would never be able to walk again.

Confident that God would see her through, they opted for the surgery. It failed. She died on the operating table as the result of complications, and the pastor took it as a personal failure. He was absolutely convinced that he was responsible for her death because he allowed her to go through the surgery. Her death became a memory that not only burned; bit scarred his life so deeply that he was unable to carry on his work as a minister. In defeat and shock, he resigned from his church, left the ministry, and began to drift from one job to another.

The parents of a four-year-old boy also found it very difficult to find healing for the self-imposed responsibility of his death. While the family was vacationing in Northern California, the dad saw a highway sign pointing to a campground. He asked his wife, "What do you think?"

"I'm so tired," she said, "let's stop."

He paused for a moment. "I'd sure like to get in a few more miles before we quit for the night." He shifted gears and rolled on down the highway.

In the back of the camper, their tired little boy crawled up into the sleeping area over the cab and went to sleep. Only a short distance down the road, there was a sudden snap as the rear axle of the camper broke. It was a freak accident that caused the camper to lurch one way and then the other before it finally turned over. The mom and dad crawled out of the tangled wreckage and frantically tried to free their trapped little boy. Moments after he was freed, the little boy died in his daddy's arms.

His funeral was one of the saddest I have ever conducted. The sight of a little boy with blond curls on his forehead resting in a four-foot casket, his *woolie* and his teddy bear cradled in one arm, absolutely tore out my heart.

What made the loss all the more difficult was that the father felt that he was totally responsible for what happened.

"It was all my fault," he reasoned. "If I had listened to my wife, we would have stopped earlier and our little boy would still be alive." Talk about painful inner struggles!

Sure, you can reason that neither the pastor whose wife died in surgery nor this father was actually responsible. Nonetheless, what happened deeply burned their memories and left wounds that could only be healed by the grace of God.

Perhaps your inner struggle is totally different, the result of having been hurt by another person. Maybe it was someone you deeply loved, someone whom you thought would never hurt you. Perhaps it was your father when you were a child, or a wife or husband later in life. Perhaps it was an angry argument with your son or daughter, broken faith with your mate, or something you did that nobody knows about except you. Whatever, it is a wound that deeply hurt you.

"A few years back," a husband wrote to me, "my wife was having an affair with another man and I caught her. I forgave her," he said, "but every time she is more than an hour late coming home, I feel she is out doing the same thing. I am trying to trust her again. Please pray for me and send me some literature on this to help me with the problem. I am trying to forget and I have forgiven her. It was about eight years ago...."

I have no doubt that every person who reads this page can sift back through the years and recall some *memories that burn,* as our friend put it, something that has created traumatic inner struggles. As the immediate trauma subsided, you probably prayed for God's forgiveness of what you did or think you did to contribute to the problem. Most of the time, you probably believe that God has forgiven you, but there may be times when you are not really sure.

Even if you know that God has forgiven you, it is certainly possible that you haven't forgiven yourself. It is quite often far more difficult to forgive ourselves than it is to accept God's forgiveness.

No matter what happened that burned your memory, there are certain steps to follow if you are going to experience emotional healing.

Guideline One

You need to understand the nature of forgiveness. No other quality, with the possible exception of love, is more needed when it comes to living harmoniously than forgiveness. The irritations of our human faults and imperfections take their toll in our daily routines. Abrasiveness causes an oyster to produce a pearl, but in people, too much abrasion produces an ulcer.

In marriage, forgiveness is the storm-wall that keeps the winds from blowing the house down. The more you love someone, the more you strive to live so that it isn't necessary to ask forgiveness. But no one is perfect, and everyone finds himself in the position of needing the only thing that can bring healing to a relationship—forgiveness.

This healing balm is a reminder of our human frailties. If we could live so that a person would neither offend nor be an offense, no one would ever have to say, "I'm sorry, forgive me." But, as we all know, no one is perfect. The individual who knows his own weaknesses and understands how forgiveness works will gladly give the priceless balm of forgiveness to another. He knows that he will eventually have to ask for the same thing.

When you forgive another person, you acknowledge an even deeper debt of gratitude than to that person. You acknowledge gratitude to God Himself. Jesus illustrated this well when He told the story of the slave who owed a rather large debt to his master. The master, out of the goodness of his heart forgave the man. However, when a fellow citizen owed a very small amount to the slave, the slave demanded that the fellow be thrown in prison until he could repay the debt (see Matthew 18:21-35).

We're like that. We are often quick to expect the other person to forgive us but we are slow to extend forgiveness to someone we think owes us. Jesus said plainly that if we do not forgive each other, neither will our Father in heaven forgive us (Matthew 6:15).

Paul, too, stressed our greater debt to God when he wrote to the Ephesians and the Colossians. He said that we must forgive each other, even as God for Christ's sake has forgiven us.

How far should you go when it comes to forgiving someone? I'm thinking of the wife of a man who got drunk nearly every Saturday night, often abusing his wife and children—verbally if not physically. One Saturday night, he arrived home in a particularly vile mood, and he found a kettle of water on the stove, the fire still on. Picking up the steaming kettle, he staggered into the bedroom and poured the water over his sleeping wife. She was taken to the hospital with severe burns covering most of her shoulders and face. When the police asked if she wished to press charges, she said, "No. I've already forgiven him."

Frankly, I hesitated to include that illustration because I don't want to leave the impression that forgiveness is a license for continued physical abuse. *Tough love* demands confrontation, and that might include separation and counseling in such a situation. The reason I used this story is that forgiveness of any kind is so contrary to the way most of us think today. Our first reactions are things like, "Give the so-and-so a taste of his own medicine!" "Divorce the lout!" "File charges and put him in the slammer!" "Besides, isn't 'an eye for an eye and a tooth for a tooth' in the Bible?"

When Absalom, David's vain son, tried to take the kingdom, King David had a forgiving spirit. Though David had to flee for his life, he bore no malice toward his son. On the contrary, when Absalom was finally apprehended by Joab and killed, David wept, "O my son Absalom! My son, my son Absalom! If only I had died instead of you—O Absalom, my son, my son!" (2 Samuel 18:33).

Peter asked Jesus the same question: "How often should I forgive my brother? Seven times?" That was really quite generous of Peter—the rabbis taught that three times was enough, and if the person did the same thing again, he was to be treated as an enemy for life. But Jesus was quite plain: "Seventy times seven!" Our tendency is to think, "A-ha! A coupon book with 490 stubs, and when they are gone, pow!" That is not the point Jesus was making. Neither seven nor 490! Jesus is telling us that there must be no end to this matter of forgiveness (see Matthew 18:21,22).

There is a lovely picture surrounding the word that the writers of Scripture used when they wrote about the necessity of forgiveness. The Greek word aphiami is usually translated *to forgive,* but it also means *to throw, or to let go.* Over time, it came to mean "to send or give up."

The word was used in legal writing when the governor forgave his subjects of back taxes that were owed to the state. It was used when criminals were forgiven by the government. This is the word frequently used in Scripture to stress the importance of learning to forgive each other. The real point is not how badly you have been hurt; rather, it is that you be willing to give up your claim to compensation for what someone has done to you.

Scripture gives many poignant illustrations of what forgiveness is. Psalm 103:12 says that when God forgives us, our sins are thrown away, as far as the east is from the west. He could have said they are as far as the north is from the south. Our sins, then would never have been more than 12,420 miles away. While there is a definite point at which one changes from north to south, or from south to north, there is no such definite point to distinguish east from west. East and west never meet.

In Micah 7, God uses the picture of the deepest sea to show us how extreme His forgiveness is. The deepest parts of the ocean on the planet are found in the Marianna trenches, where the ocean is some 35,000 feet deep—deeper than the height of Mount Everest, the highest mountain in the world. Though that is definite distance, you still would not find all of you sins and failures piled there. You could take a bathyscaphe, a little submarine with which scientists explore the depths of the ocean, and you could get to the deepest point, but you would still not find them.

Guideline Two

Be sure you have sought God's forgiveness for your own life. There are times when failures drive us to our knees, when our own behavior makes us realize that our hearts are deceptive and tricky. Scores of people have written to me to tell me how marital failures or personal tragedies caused them to realize a spiritual emptiness, and that through this they turned to God and became a Christian. This letter is typical:

"I'd like your help in learning how to let Christ into my life, to accept Him as my personal Savior. I thought I had several months ago following a severe family upheaval involving sin on my part. I had asked forgiveness of the Lord and felt I'd received it, but my wife says she cannot forgive. My wife and I love each other—she feels it would be against her principles to stay with me, but I don't want her to go. We're both miserable. Did the Lord really forgive me and is this punishment for my sins? Please help me."

Personal failures always cause us to doubt our relationship with God. If you have never received Christ as your personal Savior, you will have unrest in your heart and your emotions are bound to be troubled. If this is a picture of your life, you can pray a simple, meaningful, prayer right now:

"Heavenly Father, something is wrong with my life and I know it is the sin of my heart. I want you to forgive me and I want you to come into my life and let Jesus be my Savior right now" (see John 1:12; Acts 16:31; Romans 10:9, 13 and Titus 3:5).

If there is something specific, something you are troubled by that you know was sin in the sight of God, then remember I John 1:9: "If we confess our sins, he is faithful and just and will forgive us our sins and purify us from all unrighteousness." Mention that sin to God, confess it to Him; then, realize that He promised to forgive you, and you can be assured He has kept His word. He no longer holds that against you.

Briefly, there are four things that need to be said about God's forgiveness:

1. God's forgiveness is unconditional. You don't need to effect any self-improvement plan before you are good enough to come to God and seek His help. It isn't necessary for you to *clean up your act* first so that you are worthy of an audience with the Great King. The only obstacle is your own reluctance to come to Him. Isaiah 1:18 is still valid: "'Come now, let us reason together,' says the LORD. 'Though your sins are like scarlet, they shall be as white as snow; though they are red as crimson, they shall be like wool.'"

Jesus gave a carte blanche invitation: "...And whoever comes to me I will never drive away" (John 6:37).

2. God's forgiveness is unlimited in scope. Some people believe that God's forgiveness may cover the first offense, but after a couple or three repeats, they begin to question whether the invitation is still good. Others believe that certain deeds—abortion, adultery, fornication, homosexuality, etc.—are unforgivable. Both concepts are untrue.

Paul catalogues numerous deeds that would fall into the same category. Then he says, "And that is what some of you were. But you were washed, you were sanctified, you were justified in the name of the Lord Jesus Christ and by the Spirit of our God" (1 Corinthians 6:11). Therefore, it must be recognized that there is no limitation to the kinds of sins God will forgive when we come to Him.

3. God's forgiveness is absolute. Unlike our human memories, God wipes the slate clean, as though it had never happened.

"You mean that I will never have to give an account for the abortion that I had?" a woman who had just prayed to receive Jesus asked. Three broken marriages followed by an unwanted pregnancy had left her in a terrible state of despair. Thinking that an abortion was the only way out, she battled her conscience. She had weighed the thought of terminating the life within her body against her ability to survive as a single mother of two older children already. To add a newborn seemed too much to bear. As the nurse wheeled the gurney down the hospital corridor, glistening tears streaming down her cheeks, she cried out, "Oh, God, have I really come to this?" Right then she vowed that someway, somehow she would make the matter right with God.

"You mean that I will never have to face God again because of what I did?"

"Never again!" I explained, and I showed her what Peter says. Christ bore our sins in His body on the tree (see I Peter 2:24). The price has already been paid. That means that because God allowed Christ to be treated as we should have been treated, He can now treat us for all eternity as Christ should have been treated. That's good news!

4. God's forgiveness is redemptive. "If I asked God to forgive me before I took an overdose of drugs," a deeply disturbed woman who had given up on living asked me, "would He forgive me so I wouldn't go to hell?" This is a common question. I have sat with teenagers on occasion who say, with full understanding of what they were about to do, "I know God will forgive me so I'm going to go right ahead and do it."

One fact is often overlooked when it comes to forgiveness: When Jesus says, "I forgive you!" He also adds, "Now, go and sin no more." There is power in those words, a strength that helps an individual rise above the force or pull that threatens to drag him down again. Forgiveness brings a motive for saying, "No! I have to break this off. I just cannot continue to do this."

Guideline Three

Extend forgiveness to the one who has hurt you. Once you have squared things away with God, take a look at your relationships with other people. The next step in the process is to forgive anyone who has hurt you.

In a small, out-of-the-way cemetery in upper New York stands a tombstone bearing a single word: "FORGIVEN!" Nothing more or less, just forgiven! That single word on the otherwise unmarked grave is like a big question mark. What was forgiven? And by whom? Did some wrongdoing caused someone else to seek out the grave of the person, whose identity was eventually lost to posterity, in order to add that one word, *forgiven?*

Maybe it was a wife who, for many years, harbored resentment or perhaps even hatred toward a husband who had been unfaithful, a husband who had left her and the children for another woman whose beauty was not faded from the toil of raising children.

Perhaps it was a father who had angry words with his son. Maybe the son had packed his few belongings in a rickety suitcase and walked down the dusty road leading to the big city, only to be struck down as a prodigal who would never return. Maybe the father sought the grave so he could let the world know that he had been forgiven.

Or, perhaps, it was nothing so melodramatic as that. Perhaps someone simply wanted the world to know that he had tasted richly of God's great grace, and that he had been forgiven.

Forgiven! The very word smacks of heaven itself. Perhaps that is why some of us find it so very difficult to forgive—*to say nothing of forgetting.* Have you ever been in a situation where the hurt was so bad that you absolutely could not bring yourself to forgive? If so, you have had plenty of company through the years.

How do you overcome bitterness and hatred when you have been wronged, and when you are absolutely convinced that you cannot forgive? There was a businessman who lived in the West and had to go abroad for several years, leaving his lovely wife and three children behind. He returned, only to discover that his wife was involved with his best friend. His absence had not only cost him his wife and children; it cost him his best friend as well.

For two years hatred seethed in his heart. Try as he might, he just could not forgive them. This wrong haunted him when he slept, and it galled him when he was awake. He prayed for God to take away his hatred, but nothing happened. Finally, he went to see his pastor. He poured out the story, and his feelings of hatred, and he concluded with a question: "What must I do to forgive them?"

His pastor replied, "Nothing at all!"

The pastor went on to explain that when Jesus Christ died at Calvary, He died for our hatred, which is sin, just as He died for those acts we committed before we became Christians. He urged the man to accept the forgiveness that God had already provided. As he did that, he began to find his feelings of hatred dissipating. And he found that he could forgive them.

If you find yourself in the position of not being able to forgive another person, yet at the same time you know that God expects you to forgive just as He forgives you, then read the next few paragraphs carefully.

The first step is to come to grips with the simple fact that you can't forgive a person in your own strength. You must bring the problem to the Lord. Most of the time, we try to avoid letting God know that what we would really like to see is the offender "get it in the neck." We carry on our polite conversations with God rather than coming to the place where we admit, "God, I just can't forgive that one."

The second step is to pray for the person who has hurt you, the one you can't forgive. Does that put you on a pinnacle of virtue as you look down on the other person? Jesus prayed, "Father, forgive them...." As you pray for someone, you gradually begin to see him as a human being who is weak and frail— as totally human. Your feelings of hatred will begin to turn to pity, and finally the feelings of pity are replaced by a tenderness that allows you to forgive him.

This doesn't mean that you necessarily want to spend the rest of your life on a deserted island with the individual who has hurt you. It does mean that your stomach no longer knots when you see that person or think about him. Your lip no longer curls when his name is mentioned.

Ultimately, there needs to be confrontation with any person you have hurt, one in which you say, "I'm sorry; will you forgive me?" Ideally, the person who hurt you will come to the same place with himself. This is not a step we like. If forgiveness could be extended or received without any personal contact, it would be much easier. But eventually we all need to face uncomfortable issues in our lives if we want to grow. Facing this issue demands facing the individual with whom you have conflicts.

When you think you can't forgive someone, try to remember that forgiveness is first a matter of the will, then a matter of the emotions. Many times, if you commit to forgiveness with, "Yes, I will forgive that person; I make the decision in my head," you will find that your heart follows.

Jesus was very clear when He said that if you have conflict with another person, you are to go to him and talk to him alone. (The Greek word for *fault* in this context is harmatia. It is usually translated *sin* and this calls for confrontation, according to Matthew 18:19.) Sending a gift or letting another be your advocate may be a good gesture on your part, but it doesn't complete the transaction until you say to the person, "Please forgive me," or, "I have forgiven you, and I want you to do the same for me."

Guideline Four

You must forgive yourself. Forgiveness is like a three cornered stool in that there are three areas involved. When any one of them is missing, forgiveness is incomplete and the balance is off. Those three parts are forgiveness (1) in relationship to God, (2) in relationship to the offended person, and (3) in relationship to yourself. It is this last area, perhaps, that causes the greatest inner struggles. Undoubtedly, many people find it easier to pour out their hearts to God, to seek His forgiveness, than to forgive themselves.

Consider the burdens of these people:

I am 20 years old and have been divorced for three years and have done some bad sins. Jesus says, "If we confess our sins, He'll be faithful to forgive us," but at times I just can't forgive myself and want to die.

Another writes:

I know that what the Bible says is so true—but 15 years ago I disobeyed God's commandment and committed adultery. My husband has forgiven me, but I just can't seem to find peace of mind. I can't seem to think of anything else. What can I do?

Women are certainly not the only ones who have difficulty forgiving themselves. One man wrote:

I accepted the Lord Jesus Christ as my personal Savior some 20 years ago. It seems I have been running from myself ever since. I am the most frustrated, confused, defeated individual you will ever hear about. I have a wonderful family, wife, three boys and one daughter—all saved, everything. Yet, I am so miserable. You said something on your program this morning that may be my problem. In essence what you said was, "God has forgiven you, but you can't forgive yourself..."

Hundreds of people are like this—relatively sure that God has forgiven them, but unable to let themselves off the hook. If you are like that, ask yourself a somewhat philosophical question: "What right do I have to refuse to forgive myself when God has forgiven me?" We'd all agree, theoretically, that there is no right. Your failing to forgive yourself destroys your peace of mind and it further diminishes your effectiveness because you bear an incredible burden of guilt. This is not a guilt that God intended for you to carry.

Guideline Five

Give the bitterness of that memory to Jesus. Why should you carry the burden of a memory that burns or scars when Jesus already died for that very burden? Simply put, that is not your responsibility.

When I talk to people about whether or not they have a right to hold a grudge against themselves, I have often followed up with a second rather ludicrous question: "Are you greater than God is?" They usually smile and say, "I see how ridiculous it is." It is because you do care about the effect your actions have on yourself and others that you punish yourself. But, as we have already seen, failing to forgive yourself robs you of peace of mind, destroys your ability to function properly, and certainly saps you of spiritual vitality. In a very real sense, by continuing to hold your sin against yourself, you render what Christ did ineffective. What you are saying is that you can bear the guilt of your sin, but your sin is what He bore long ago so you wouldn't have to.

You need to take positive action to rid yourself of that guilt once and for all, to get things into perspective. First, in your mind's eye, picture Jesus as He hung on the cross with all the suffering and loneliness He endured. It is not a very pleasant picture. There is an inscription posted above Him.

The inscription that was placed on Jesus' cross didn't make the Jews very happy. It read, "This is Jesus, the King of the Jews," and it was written in Hebrew, Greek, and Aramaic (Matthew 27:37). The very act of hanging a sign during a crucifixion was part of the crucifixion ritual instituted by the Romans. In order to make the person more of a public example, the Romans would write the crime for which the person was being executed on parchment or papyrus. They placed it on the cross so that all who passed by would know why that person was executed.

Now, think about the memory that burns, the sin or deed that troubles you, as if it were written on a piece of parchment and affixed to the cross as the crime for which Jesus died. Picture the blood that flowed from His wounds covering that writing until it is obliterated forever.

Paul painted the picture of our sins being obliterated like that when he wrote to the Colossians: "When you were dead in your sins and in the uncircumcision of your sinful nature, God made you alive with Christ. He forgave us all our sins, having canceled the written code, with its regulations, that was against us and that stood opposed to us; he took it away, nailing it to the cross" (Colossians 2:13,14).

This is not mental *hocus-pocus*, or conjuring up images that do not exist but that you wish would happen, like something New Age adherents call *visualization*. Viewing yourself and your sin from God's perspective is part of faith. No wonder the author of Hebrews wrote, "Faith is being sure of what we hope for and certain of what we do not see" (Hebrews 11:1).

Another way you can help rid your memory of the bitterness that burns your soul is to sit down and write out the memory in detail. Write out the sordid details in longhand, but do it in private. Now take the memorandum and crumple it up in a ball. In your mind's eye, picture Jesus standing in front of you. See the nail-scarred hands taking the memorandum from you, so that you will never face it again. As you do this, literally give the memory to Him. Remember, from God's vantage point, the sin is already gone. Forgiven! He gave us a promise: "I, even I, am he who blots out your transgressions, for my own sake, and remembers your sins no more" (Isaiah 43:25).

It may help to touch a match to what you have written. As the flames lick it up, remind yourself that you, as a conscious act of the will, gave that memory to Jesus. Then, leave it in His hands.

Guideline Six

Refuse to let your mind dwell on the memory that burns. Some folks live with constant bitterness and heartache because they cling to the shattered fragments of a life that went to pieces. At every opportunity, they tell their story—and if an opportunity doesn't come up, they'll make one! Eventually, their friends no longer want to hear it and avoid them. Loneliness only compounds the hurt. If God has forgiven you, and if you have forgiven yourself, and if you have forgiven those who hurt you, refuse to let your mind dwell on the matter. Satan often defeats us by bringing to our minds things that have been forgiven and must be forgotten.

Guideline Seven

Replace the memory that burns with the Word of God. There is therapeutic healing in the Word of God itself. The Holy Spirit uses the Word to bring restoration and healing to burned out emotions. Dave Wilkerson, author of the book, *The Cross and the Switchblade,* said that the most effective therapy for a person who has burned out his mind with drugs is to program his mind with God's Word, the Bible. This brings psychological and spiritual healing. He is not alone in that claim. And it has been my experience that the same applies not only to individuals whose minds have been dulled by drugs but also to individuals who have burned out emotionally.

Guideline Eight

Cooperate with the Holy Spirit in your healing. Be very certain of this fact: when you search the catalog of virtues or characteristics of the Spirit-filled life (Galatians 5:22,23), you will not find bitterness listed among them. You will, however, find it characterized in the description of the flesh immediately preceding it. Simply put, bitterness is not from the Lord, and your cooperation with the Holy Spirit to allow God to touch your life is very important.

It is the nature of Satan to ensnare, deceive, and destroy while it is the nature of God to liberate, and bring restoration and healing. It is a defective theology that believes God is interested only in extending forgiveness to a person while leaving his emotional life stunted and twisted by memories that burn. Emotional healing has to be part of the redemptive plan of the God. He told His children right out, "I am the Lord that healeth thee" (Exodus 15:26, KJV). David blessed the Lord, "who forgives all your sins and heals all your diseases" (Psalms 103:3). This has to include the healing of the memory and emotions, and not just the physical body.

If you mean business about finding God's healing power for your emotions and the memories that burn, and you still have not found relief, I suggest that you take the next step, which is outlined in James 5:14. Call upon the elders of your local congregation and ask them to anoint you with oil and to pray for emotional healing. It isn't necessary to share the details of what troubles you, but it is necessary to have someone else pray for you in order to have complete healing.

If you are not in a church, if there are none near you, have several other Christians join you and ask them to pray according to the outline of James 5. You may be thinking, "Well, I can pray for myself." Yes, you can. But there is much to be said for the power of corporate prayer. There are times when you don't have the faith to believe God for yourself. You are the one who has taken it on the chin emotionally, and you might feel that you can't get it all together on your own. Praying with another person will compound your faith.

How is that? I'm not sure that I can explain the *how* of it, but the *why* of it was laid down by Jesus: "Again, I tell you that if two of you on earth agree about anything you ask for, it will be done for you by my Father in heaven. For where two or three come together in my name, there am I with them" (Matthew 18:19,20).

For far too long, many churches have looked the other way when it comes to recognizing the power of God in healing the body, the emotions, and the soul. Perhaps it is because of the quacks and professional *healers* who have prostituted the power of God for their own selfish purposes. But, even so, we must assume the privilege, as well as the responsibility, of ministering to the needs of the whole man. We must redeem the spiritual birthright and heritage that we have in Jesus Christ.

Guideline Nine

Begin praising God for bringing restoration and healing to your life. When fire swept through Laguna Canyon near our office, one of the properties destroyed was the Hortense Miller Garden, a botanical garden containing more than 2,000 varieties of plants and flowers. The place was a veritable paradise of beautiful flowers and greenery. The fire, of course, blackened the hillside and left its ugly scars. Disaster? Yes! That's what people called it and rightly so. Yet, today, months later, the hills are alive with the beauty of wild flowers that have not been seen in the area for between thirty and one hundred years. You see, years ago, before the area was converted into a garden, wild flowers covered the hillside. But these gave way to the domestic plants and shrubs that soon took over the sunlight and snagged the nourishment from the soil. The seeds of the wild flowers, however, lay in the ground—some thirty to forty years, some even seventy-five to one hundred years. They were dormant but not dead. Then came the fire, a disaster from the human standpoint. It burned most things to the ground, allowing the sunlight and the rain to penetrate the dormant wild seeds. They then sprang up in resurrection beauty.

"I wasn't too happy about [the fire]," Mrs. Miller, owner of the garden, said, "but, I think this is exciting." Today, it's different from the formal, more stately garden that existed before the fire, but the beauty is still there—rearranged by God's own hand. What appeared to us to be a disaster gave the area a different sort of beauty, one which could only be produced by the hand of God Himself.

There is a difference between a Christian and the person who considers life a disorganized and disconnected move of fate. The Christian knows—*or should know*—that God's purpose and design is behind every event, even though he cannot see the pattern at the time. The Christian looks for the wild flowers after the fire, and he can accept the fact that God is working all things after the pattern of His will (see Ephesians 1:11; Romans 8:28).

Let Him work in your life. Begin to thank Him for the restoration and healing that can follow a fire. Then, begin to look for the flowers that can transform the blackened landscape of life into a wild and colorful garden.

The wild flowers are sure to come.

Discussion Questions:

Alicia was happily married and the mother of two darling girls. After ten years of marriage, her husband Jim began to grow distant. He spent more and more time away from home, and when he was home he usually escaped into the TV. Alicia's world collapsed when Jim announced that he had never really loved her, that he was tired of living a lie, and that he wanted a divorce so he could marry another woman who worked in his office. Alicia now lies awake nights, replaying the fact that she was pregnant when she and Jim were married. Even though Jim hadn't wanted to get married at first, they did, and he seemed happy until he dropped his bomb.

1. What are some of the ways Alicia might blame herself? What are two things she can do in order to deal with the pain and the betrayal so that the result is not bitterness?

2. Think of one thing that used to be a memory that burns but is no longer so. What was the process you went through in order to get rid of the bitterness or guilt?

3. What is one memory that is still burning into your mind, either something you did or something that was done to you? What are three things you can do—either what has worked for you in the past or something you learned from this chapter—to start the healing process?

This will hurt....

Replaying the emotional tapes over and over in your mind will only compound guilt, frustration, anger, and any other emotion. It will keep you focused assigning blame. It will hurt to hold your bitterness to you because bitterness eats at your soul like acid and spills out onto other people.

This will help....

Many people find that some pain is too big to face alone. You might want to get counseling, or talk to a good friend. It will help to remember that healing is a process and that it will take time.

You can try this exercise: Write out exactly how you feel—put all of your anger and bitterness down on paper. Then, light a match and touch it to the paper. As you watch the flames erase the words, remind yourself that you can let go of the feelings they expressed. Ask God to help you leave the ashes with Him.

CHAPTER FIVE

The Inner Struggle Of Anger

Is it bad to get mad?

A certain Illinois businessman gave a porter a large tip asking that the porter be sure to put him off the train the next morning at 5A.M., at Deerpark. He explained that he had a very important engagement and that he was a very sound sleeper and feared he would not wake up.

"Yes, sir!" replied the porter, "I can take care of it for you!"

But at 9A.M. the next morning, the businessman awakened to discover he was still on the train and was at least 200 miles beyond Deerpark. It was a very angry man who found the porter and gave him a verbal tongue-lashing, throwing in a few words that hadn't been used since his Navy days, before he stomped off the train.

"That absolutely has to be the maddest man I have ever seen," replied the conductor who happened to be standing nearby.

"Boy, if you think he was mad," replied the porter, you should have seen how angry the man was I put off the train this morning at 5 A.M.!"

We chuckle at the incident, but the number of people, today, who allow anger to get the best of them is no laughing matter.

Anger Is On The Increase

Displays of anger, both public and private, are on the increase today, according to Dr. James Comer, Professor of Psychiatry at Yale University. He says, "This definitely is an 'angry age'—much more so than at any time in history."[1]

If you question that displays of anger are on the increase, notice what happens when somebody cuts in front of another car at the gas pump, or what happens when somebody pushes somebody in a crowded elevator, or steps in front of somebody in a checkstand line in a grocery store. Tempers flare and fast! Most of us have grown up feeling that anger is a potentially dangerous emotion, and that any display of anger is always wrong, but is it really?

Is It Bad To Get Mad?

Surprising as it is to some folks, the Bible has a great deal to say about anger, or strong wrath. In the Old Testament alone there are 455 references to anger; of those, 375 are references to God Himself. Many of those references are in relationship to His own people, Israel, who refused to follow the direction of their heavenly Father, and the result was that God was displeased, yes, no less than angry with them because of it.

In the New Testament there are many references to anger and how to cope with it. Jesus was angry with His disciples on several occasions because of their refusal to believe Him. He became angry with the Pharisees because of the hardness of their hearts and their hypocrisy. "Whitened sepulchers full of dead men's bones" was Jesus' description of them. His anger was obvious when He overturned the tables of the money changers and the benches of those selling doves in the temple. Picking up a whip He drove them out. "My house will be called a house of prayer," he said, "but you are making it a 'den of robbers'" (Matthew 21:13).

The Bible makes it clear that anger, like a scalpel in the hands of a skilled surgeon, is amoral in itself; it can either be harmful and wrong, or used properly can be a powerful motive for character and integrity.

The writers of Scripture refer to strong anger as "wrath," and almost always it is referred to in a negative context. Paul wrote, "For God did not appoint us to suffer wrath but to receive salvation through our Lord Jesus Christ" (1 Thessalonians 5:9). Wrath—strong anger— usually works against us, provoking us to do things we later regret. "For the wrath of man worketh not the righteousness of God" (James 1:20, KJV).

The Bible clearly differentiates between *being angry* and *remaining angry.* "In your anger do not sin" was Paul's guideline to the Ephesians (see Ephesians 4:26). Therefore, it is how you handle anger that determines whether it is right or wrong.

Why is it that we are an angry, uptight generation? To make it personal, why do you allow your temper to flare on occasion? Why should we be angry, when we have so much that previous generations didn't have? For a few minutes, think with me about some of the factors that produce the gunpowder of emotional outbursts which often explode at the slightest spark of provocation.

1. Stress produces anger. We live busier lives today than at any time in recent history, and tension is the result. Like the string of a violin that is tightened and tightened until it snaps, we load our schedules tighter and tighter until we explode in a burst of anger, and then ask ourselves, "Why did I allow myself to get so mad?" It's simple—you had too much crowded into a short span of time, and then you feel guilty because you are convinced that "spiritual folks" just don't get angry. But you did, and you dislike yourself because of it.

You are trying to do what Jesus Himself could not do—live without proper rest and relaxation. He told His disciples to "come apart and rest awhile" after their labors, but you don't allow yourself time to do that. But, if you don't learn to "come apart and rest awhile," you'll just come apart, and you won't like it when it happens. We will take an indepth look at stress and how it affects our lives in chapter nine.

2. Frustration produces outbursts of anger. I know. It happened to me recently and, while I like to think of myself as a *pretty much in control* sort of person, my response surprised me. I was returning from an overseas period of ministry and stopped in Korea for a couple of days of relaxation and shopping with my wife.

Not wanting to run out of money, I had carefully allocated what I needed for the brief stay, even down to the remaining cost of the taxi, the tip for the porters who carried the suitcases, and enough to buy lunch before our departure. Making sure that I didn't mix up the amounts, I had tucked the taxi money in my shirt pocket, and folded two ¥1,000 notes— about $1.30 each—for the porters.

Everything went according to the plan until I stepped up to pay for our lunch. As I began to search my wallet, I realized that I had mistakenly mixed up the two bills and had given the porters the ¥10,000 notes which were supposed to pay for lunch (about $13.00 each). That generous tip may have made their day, but it didn't mine. I was so angry with myself that I stomped my foot on the floor. As I was greeted with curious stares from the folks lined up behind me, I began to realize how ridiculous for me to be upset over that issue. I was wasting a good deal more than twenty-six dollars worth of adrenaline on the situation. I quickly remembered a VISA card and paid for my meal, feeling very sheepish. My anger with myself was the result of frustration because I had made a mistake.

Failure to see your expectations met does the same thing—whether it is in your marriage or in the lives of your children, failure to get the grade you deserved in a class at school, failure to receive the promotion you felt you deserved—all of these and other such irritations produce frustration. When there is no relief valve, frustration can build into anger.

Says Yale psychiatrist James Comer, "People have a sense that the world is closing in on them, that there are too many people around and that they are getting ripped off. We feel powerless. All of a sudden, we're beginning to doubt that anybody can do anything about our problems, and we are angry. We explode in frustration."[2]

We all can't afford to deal with frustration as a friend of mine did, who took his trail bike into the mountains hunting. When it refused to run, John started tinkering with it, but it still wouldn't start. The longer he worked on it, the more he thought about missing his hunt and the madder he got. After enduring as much as his patience would stand, he drew his .45 pistol and proceeded to blast the bike into oblivion and then push it off a cliff. Sometimes we'd like to do that, but it just isn't economically feasible.

3. Personal affronts produce anger. Somebody tells a Polish joke and you happen to have parents who were born in

Warsaw; or they call you a "gringo," or a "Jap." You take it as an insult to your race and you allow your temper to flare.

I know how you feel. I arrived in an African country where I was to speak, and having had enough of being *cooped up* on a plane, I was ready to get off as soon as the plane hit the ground. I was the first one out the door and, subsequently, was the first person to arrive at customs.

I handed my passport to the custom officer who lazily took it and started to process it; but, when a couple of nationals arrived, he pushed my passport to the back of his desk and processed theirs first, I stood there and waited rather patiently, but each time a national approached, my passport got shoved back further, and I grew a little hotter under the collar. I had the good sense to realize I was a guest in the country and kept my mouth shut, but it made me realize that personal injustices are some of the reasons that people allow tempers to get out of hand.

4. The violation of your rights produces anger. In marriage, a man expects certain things of his wife, and she, in turn, also expects certain things of her husband. Those expectations—which may not be perceived the same way by a husband and wife—are generally the result of seeing certain things in the home in which a person grew up. When those expectations are not realized, or the rights and privileges which one of you extends to the other are not returned, irritation turns into anger.

We consider our being slighted as an attack on our person, and we aren't going to sit there and let somebody walk over us, no sir! We're going to stand up for our rights (even if it blows a marriage apart)! You may win the argument but lose a friend or possibly a husband or wife in the process.

5. Situations which counter your value system produce anger. A study of the life of Jesus indicates that most of His

anger was occasioned by situations which were wrong, and He did something about them. Call it "righteous indignation," or whatever you like, but we need more of it.

Newspapers recently told of a woman driving down a street when she saw two muggers riffling the pockets of a man who had his hands in the air. She stopped, sensing it was a hold-up, and began to honk the horn of her car. This occasioned a blast of a 12-gauge shotgun at her car as the robbers made their get-away. But undaunted, Mrs. Silbert leaned on the horn of her car and trailed the suspects, who soon crashed into a parked car and were arrested by police. She told a reporter, "I just said to myself, I'm not going to let them get away with that! I guess I just got mad."

Learning To Cope With Anger

While anger is potentially a negative emotion, and used improperly can create lots of havoc, used properly (as in the true story which I just related) anger works for our good and that of society in general. The following are five guidelines which you can use in learning to cope with anger in such a way that makes it take its rightful place in your life.

Guideline One

Learn to cope with anger by avoiding stressful situations. Naturally, you can't avoid them all, but you can some. Organize yourself so you eliminate pressured situations that evoke anger, like getting up too late consistently, which means you drive too fast to work, or failing to leave for the airport in time, or planning your time so tightly that the slightest change of schedule really angers you. Planning ahead can eliminate some of those situations that are apt to trigger your temper.

Guideline Two

Learn to cope with anger by putting the circumstances in perspective. When you start to feel the slow burn, stop and ask yourself, "Is the situation really worth the emotional stress and strain to get angry?" Maybe you need to ask, "Is that person worth losing my temper over?" The problem with too many people today is that they are temperamental—too much temper and not enough mental.

Vance Havner reminds us, "Any bulldog can whip a skunk, but sometimes it just ain't worth it." He's right. Is it worth the risk of getting fired to tell your boss what you think of him? What does it do to your wife and children? So what if I tipped the porters ten times the amount that I intended! Life is going to go on, and a hundred years from now it won't matter. And besides, as my wife suggested, maybe God used that gift to meet a tremendous need in their lives! Who knows?

Put the circumstances into perspective and you'll learn that over the long haul, it isn't worth the frustration and the turmoil in your life that losing your temper occasions.

Guideline Three

Learn to discipline your emotions. James, the half-brother of Jesus, wrote, "My dear brothers, take note of this: Everyone should be quick to listen, slow to speak and slow to become angry" (James 1:19). Today, we are slow to listen, quite ready to speak, and prone to anger. There are times, however, when the Kingdom of God as well as your personal life is better served by your learning to discipline your speech and keep your temper under control.

A 6'9" basketball player by the name of Baynard Forrest discovered this when he was playing for Athletes in Action. "If I can't control my temper out there [on the basketball court]," Forrest told a reporter, "I'm not going to be a great witness. I know it gets real tough under the basket and that hard, physical contact is part of the game. But, I've got to retain my cool if I'm going to be a Christian example." Enough said!

I'm thinking of a Seattle father of three who was driving home at the end of a busy day when a car cut in front of him. Angered, he accelerated and passed the car, cutting in front of him, just as the other driver had done. Now both drivers were angry, and the one who initiated the exchange, pulled his car alongside the father of three, took a gun from beneath the seat, and pulled the trigger, killing the man instantly.

He vented his temper, but at great cost! When someone annoys you and you feel the ire rising within, you've got to ask yourself, "Is this guy worth it? Am I willing to stoop to his or her level?" You've got to remind yourself of the fact that you are wasting an awful lot of adrenaline over an issue that just isn't worth it. Far too often when we are bothered by something our responses are emotional "overkill!" It's like shooting a fly with a .45 instead of using a fly swatter. Far too much emotional energy is expended.

At times we need to be more like the father of a three-year old who was shopping in a department store. The dad would make comments, "Easy, Albert!" "Slow down, boy." "Get a handle on yourself, 'ol buddy." A bystander overheard the father and said, "I'm a child psychologist, and I'd like to commend you on the way you handle your son Albert."

"My son, nothing!" replied the man. "My name is Albert!"

Guideline Four

Vent your emotions so anger doesn't breed in your heart. How? Four ways are worth mentioning. Physical exercise is a great way—you literally run the stress out of your system by jogging, swimming, calisthenics, walking, or whatever.

Another way to vent your emotions properly is through music. Leonard Bernstein once said, "It's a remarkably lucky thing to be able to storm your way through a Beethoven Symphony. Think of the amount of rage you can get out. If you exhibited that on the streets or in an interpersonal relationship, you'd be thrown in jail. Instead, you're applauded for it." Better to beat a drum or the keyboard of a piano than be tempted to beat your kids or your wife.

Vent your emotions through painting as you transfer bursts of emotion to canvas rather than to the members of your family.

Vent emotions through prayer as I suggested in the chapter on emotions and how to handle them.

Guideline Five

Learn to cope with anger by eliminating stressful situations which you can change. This guideline, of necessity, will not apply to everything that disturbs you, but if there is a situation which constantly irritates you, and you **CAN** do something about it, then **DO** it. Perhaps, it means changing churches rather than staying where you have been for the last twenty-five years and becoming bitter and angry. Perhaps, it means going ahead and buying a new car instead of coping with the frustration of trying to keep a car running when it should have passed from the scene a long time ago. Perhaps, it means changing jobs rather than staying where you have been bypassed for promotion. But, of course, there are those times when we can't change things and must, of necessity, pray that God will give us the grace to accept what we cannot change.

Training Your Temper

Anger is a strong emotion, but it is neither good or bad. It's how you handle it that puts it in one column or the other. When you get mad, one of three things will happen:

1. You will stay angry. A lot of people are like that. They are always mad. They are like a thunder cloud about to storm. Their thermostats run at 210°—they are always just under the boiling point. They retain deep-seated hostilities that may go clear back to childhood, and clearly, anger such as I've just described is harmful.

2. You rationalize your anger, and never get angry when you should. What could produce moral character and integrity produces vacillation and indifference.

3. When you get angry, you can learn how to make your anger work for you, and this is the right thing.

Ever wonder how to be good and mad without being bad? This section contains at least four guidelines that will help you accomplish that objective. They are based on Paul's direction to the Ephesians when he wrote, "Be angry, and sin not: let not the sun go down upon your wrath" (Ephesians 4:26; KJV).

Guideline One

Be angry with the right person. Too often we take out hostilities on the wrong person— usually an innocent one who happened to be at the wrong place, at the wrong time. Like this situation: You are really angry with your boss, but not having the courage to confront him, you come home all hot and bothered. When you get to the garage, you notice that your child's bicycle is not in its proper place and you instinctively yell at him. Sure, you told him at least a dozen times to put his bike away when he finishes riding, but the intensity of your feelings goes way beyond the seriousness of the situation.

Misplaced aggression is one of the prime reasons for child abuse and physical violence among adults. Being unable to handle anger on the job, we vent the feelings on the weak and helpless victims of our aggression who generally can't or won't fight back.

This is why Jesus instructed us to go to the person with whom we have a problem and deal with the problem on a one-to-one basis (see Matthew 18:15, and following). This way we allow our anger to be dispelled in a right way with the right person.

Guideline Two

Be angry for the right cause. Part of our problem today is that we are angry over the wrong causes. What should evoke "moral indignation" or old-fashioned anger is met with indifference, and what angers us should be met with discipline and tact. There is a time and a place for anger, as Ecclesiastes 3:1-8 states.

Jesus gave us an example when He became angry with the money changers who had turned the temple into a den of merchandise. "Jesus entered the temple area and drove out all who were buying and selling there. He overturned the tables of the money changers and the benches of those selling doves. 'It is written,' he said to them, 'My house will be called a house of prayer, but you are making it a 'den of robbers'" (Matthew 21:12,13). Jesus was angry and rightly so! We need to get angry at the inroads of pornography, indecency in public life, corruption in government, and such issues today—at least as angry with situations such as these as we become when our favorite television program is pre-empted by a football game we're not interested in watching.

Guideline Three

Be angry for the right duration of time. That's the summation of Paul's advice, "Don't let the sun go down on your wrath." His advice is to get it out of your system. Say it as kindly as possible, but get it off your chest. Don't carry it over to the next day. What happens when we fail to heed Paul's advice? Dr. Leo Madow, a physician, has documented the harmful effect of lingering anger. Unvented anger, he says, produces a vast array of physical problems from arthritis to asthma, from urinary disorders to the common cold. It also produces a vast spectrum of psychological problems—all of which could be avoided by this third guideline.

Guideline Four

Be angry in the right way. If anger can be directed against the problem rather than the person who has created the problem, it becomes constructive and positive. But, when you put your fist through the wall, or punch your brother-in-law who owes you money, you have only created a worse problem—not only your wallet hurts, but your fist will the next day. Jesus was angry in the right way by doing something constructive—He eliminated the money-changers from the temple; and you will find that usually those who are wrong will back down and flee just as did Jesus' adversaries when He drove them from the temple.

Yes, there is a time and a place for everything, and by following these guidelines you will discover that your temper, which could destroy your marriage or your job, can work for you. With God's help, you can learn to control it instead of allowing it to defeat you. You can win those inner struggles.

Discussion Questions:

You are driving home on the freeway at he end of the day when a smart-aleck in a battered up van cuts in front of you, forcing you to slam on your brakes or rear end the guy. You lean on your horn expressing your feelings, and the offending driver turns around and gives you the finger.

1. Name two times you have been angry recently. How did you cope with anger in each case? Was one situation easier to resolve than the other? If so, what did you do differently in each case?

2. Name an everyday situation about which you are angry regularly. What are some steps you can take to cope with that anger?

3. Name one situation about which you have been angry for a long time. Are you angry with the right person? Are you angry at the right cause? Has your anger lasted too long considering the situation? Are you being angry in the right way? What are some ways you can work to resolve that anger?

This will hurt....

Many times, our natural reaction is to try to put the other person in his place when we are offended or insulted. We might want to step on the accelerator, zip around the guy in the van, and cut him off. If we can make eye contact with a solid and fuming glare as we pass, we feel even more vindicated. All this really does for us, though, is to make us more angry and cause more stress. It will hurt if we keep thinking about the situation, tell people about it all day, or add it to our list of things that have gone wrong in life.

This will help....

Escalating a situation rarely helps. Keep things in perspective. As Vance Havner put it, "Any bulldog can whip a skunk, but sometimes it just ain't worth it." An old proverb says, "He who overcomes another is strong, but he who overcomes himself is mighty!" It will help to take a deep breath and give yourself time to think about the situation. It will help to think through the guidelines given in this chapter about coping with anger. It is possible to lose your time, your energy, even your life over things that are not worth it.

Notes

[1]James Comer, "How To Control Your Anger," U. S. News and World Report, October 10, 1977, p. 53.

[2]Ibid. p. 57.

CHAPTER SIX

The Inner Struggle Of Worry

Lyndon Johnson once asked an elderly lady how she was getting along. She replied, "Fine!" Then, she explained:

When I walks, I walks slowly,

When I sits, I sits loosely.

When I sees a worry coming on me,

I just lies down and goes to sleep.

Everyone, however, is not capable of doing that. I received a letter that expresses a common struggle Christians have: "I'm a Christian, and I know I shouldn't worry, but I do. Is there anything I can do to overcome this?" Indeed, there is! That's what this chapter is about. Worry is the label we use for a lot of our inner struggles. Some of these struggles we can talk about, and some are so intensely personal that it is very difficult to describe them, even to our best friend.

It seems that nearly everybody worries about something these days. We worry about the weather, our health, what may happen in the world. We worry about Israel's dropping "the bomb" on Syria, or what the Arabs may do to precipitate another crisis in the Middle East. Single folks worry about getting married, and some of the married folks worry about staying that way.

Even kids are getting in on the worry game, according to psychologists. It is nothing unusual for a ten-year-old to show up with ulcers because of the social and home pressures he is under. Whether you are eight or eighty, your stomach will keep score when you are worried. It's the way God made you. Inevitably, your body becomes tense, muscles tighten, and you feel its deadly result.

Worry has become a growing industry. Our inability to cope with worry sends us to psychiatrists, psychologists, therapists, and counselors. Searching for an answer to the problem, thousands of people have bought into a variety of cures ranging from pop-psychology and new age teaching to self-help books. There is a wide spectrum of proposed *solutions* from cults to Bible-oriented teaching.

One of the strange things about worry is that it seems to take as many professing Christians as non-believers among its victims. How many Christians do you know who are known for their smooth brow and calm temperament?

Now, of course, if there is no God who controls the affairs of your life, then you had better worry about the future; the success or failure of your life hinges on your efforts alone! But, on the other hand, if there is a God in heaven who will direct and guide you, if there is a God who hears and answers prayer, you waste your time and dissipate a tremendous amount of energy when you worry.

The Bible addresses this issue head on. When you have time, look up the references to anxiety or worry in a concordance. Most of the passages you'll find listed there are from one of two primary spokesmen: Jesus and the Apostle Paul. Jesus said more about worry than all the other writers of Scripture put together.

Among the issues He addresses are what we are going to eat or drink, or what we will wear (see Matthew 6:25-34). His followers should also not worry about what to say when antagonism against them brings them into conflict with government authorities (see Matthew 10:19). He told Martha that she was "worried and upset about many things"(Luke 10:41), but that those things were not worth her worried energy.

But it was Paul, the second most vocal spokesman, who clarified the difference between worry and concern. Concern, Paul taught, is legitimate. Concern for your health or physical safety, or concern for people may motivate you to take the steps necessary for well-being. Worry, on the other hand, is the persistent, nagging, debilitating concern over something you can generally do nothing about.

Part of the reason it is hard to distinguish between the two is that the line that exists between concern and worry is very fine. Paul says that an unmarried man is *concerned*—the same word usually translated as worry—about the Lord's work whereas a married person is concerned about pleasing his or her mate (1 Corinthians 7:32-34). The body of Christ is to show concern, but not worry, for each other (1 Corinthians 12:25). Concern should be a positive force resulting in our enrichment and betterment.

Now, let's read beyond the headline and notice some of the fine print in what Jesus and Paul say about worry. In the Sermon on the Mount, Jesus said, "Therefore I tell you, do not worry about your life, what you will eat or drink; or about your body, what you will wear. Is not life more important than food, and the body more important than clothes?" (Matthew 6:25). Then I can just see Jesus gesture toward the birds that were flitting over the fields surrounding Galilee as He said, "Look at the birds of the air; they do not sow or reap or store away in barns, and yet your heavenly Father feeds them. Are you not much more valuable than they?" (Matthew 6:26).

Worry is completely needless, Jesus said, a conviction that few of us have today. Worry accomplishes nothing positive. Instead, it deprives us of needed sleep. Like a broken record that plays the same scratchy track over and over again, worry occupies our minds with unproductive thoughts. It keep us from seeking out productive solutions, and it never changes anything.

Worry Is Needless Because Of God's Care

Immediately before His death and resurrection, Jesus met with His disciples in the Upper Room and there gave them what could be considered His last instructions regarding the future. He said, "Stop letting your hearts be troubled [and that spells worry]. You believe in God, believe also in me" (John 14:1, my translation). The message in all of Scripture is that worry is needless because there is a God in heaven who is fully in control of the situation and has demonstrated a personal concern for your life.

Paul zeroed in on this universal problem of worry when he wrote these words to the Philippians: "Don't worry about anything; instead, pray about everything; tell God your needs and don't forget to thank him for his answers" (Philippians 4:6, LB). If you do this you will experience God's peace, which is far more wonderful than the human mind can understand. His peace will keep your thoughts and your hearts quiet and at rest as you trust in Christ Jesus" (Philippians 4: 6,7, LB). Paul's antidote is simple: "Don't worry about anything—pray about everything."

This means, quite simply put, that you can take the everyday needs of your life to God and trust Him for a solution. A mother who is concerned about the social adjustment of her six-year-old can make this a matter of prayer rather than worry about it. A father who is concerned about the possibility of his job running out, which means unemployment and insufficient income for the family, can make this a matter of prayer rather than a debilitating anxiety. A teenager who is waiting to hear about being accepted into college can trust God rather than worry.

By its very act, worry says that you don't believe God is big enough, or powerful enough, or willing enough to do anything about the needs of your life; therefore, you yourself had better be concerned. When you find yourself worrying, ask yourself if that's what you actually believe?

Worry Is Needless Because Of The Providence Of God

I believe it was primarily for this reason that Jesus was so hard on those who worry. He knew that God is all-powerful, and He understood that our Heavenly Father is honor-bound to keep His word. The law and the prophets clearly teach that about God, truths the disciples should have known. Moses wrote, "God is not a man, that he should lie, nor a son of man, that he should change his mind. Does he speak and then not act? Does he promise and not fulfill?" (Numbers 23:19).

Simply put, Jesus believed that God would fulfill His responsibility to His children; therefore, the relationship of a son with the Father should be that of trust, not fear or even duty. Mark records the prayer of Jesus from the garden of Gethsemane: "'Abba, Father,' he said, 'everything is possible for you. Take this cup from me. Yet not what I will, but what you will'" (Mark 14:36).

The fact that God has a will for us that goes far beyond our limited vision and understanding is part of what we call the providence of God. It is embodied in Proverbs 3:5,6, where we find these words, "Trust in the Lord with all thine heart; and lean not unto thine own understanding. In all thy ways acknowledge him, and he shall direct thy paths" (Proverbs 3: 5,6, KJV). Those last words, "He shall direct thy paths," are God's promise of guidance no matter how limited your understanding or how dark the world in which you live.

When I think of God's providential guidance, I think of Joseph, who was sold into slavery by his own brothers. It was a difficult situation that appeared to be hopeless from a human perspective. Then, from the lowly position of a slave in Pharaoh's house, Joseph rose to the position of Egypt's prime minister. And Joseph could say, "… ye thought evil against me; but God meant it unto good" (Genesis 50:20, KJV).

Do you have that assurance when things go wrong in your household? When you have more bills than you have money, or illness strikes in your family, do you have the deep, settled confidence that God works all things after the counsel of His own will, as Paul tells us in Ephesians 1:11?

This doesn't mean that you will never face financial problems. It is a promise, however, that those problems will not overwhelm you. It doesn't mean that you will not face personal problems, but it does mean that you need not be crushed by them. It means that God will be with you as you face the battles of life.

Worry Is Futile

Jesus indicated this by asking, "Who of you by worrying can add a single hour to his life?" (Matthew 6:27). A soldier who determined that worry wouldn't get the best of him carried the following on a little card in his helmet:

> "One of two things is certain. Either you are at the front or else behind the lines. If at the front, of two things one is certain. Either you are exposed to danger or in a safe place. If exposed to danger, of two things one is certain, you are either wounded or not. If wounded, you will either recover or die. IF YOU DIE, YOU CAN'T WORRY...SO WHY WORRY NOW?"

That soldier had wisely come to recognize the futility of worry. Most of the things you worry about never materialize. That was confirmed by the findings of a panel of psychologists who met together to study the effects of worry. They concluded that 40 percent of what we worry about never happens. Thirty percent of our worries are about past events—things that have already happened which you cannot change, such as how well you did on last Friday's test, or how you did in the sales presentation you made last week. Another twelve percent of our worries are concerned with needless health concerns—the "what if's."

I know one woman who majored on those concerns. She said she always felt bad when she felt good because she knew eventually she would feel bad again. She did...eventually! About ten percent of our worries involve trifling things of absolutely no consequence. Only eight percent of our worries, according to the research of that panel of psychologists, are valid areas of concern. As Mark Twain wisely observed, "I am an old man and have known my troubles, but most of them never happened!"

We have lost sight of the great truth of God's providence and His watchcare for His children. We quote Romans 8:28, "And we know that in all things God works for the good of those who love him...," while at the same time we allow our stomachs to knot and we worry about the very things we have not bothered to pray about. Ulcers become the badges of our faith, and Maalox becomes the wine of our defunct communion with God.

George Lyons wrote, "Worry is the interest paid by those who borrow trouble." The senseless thing about worry is that it does nothing to change the future or what might—but probably will not—happen. What it does do is effectively neutralize our productivity today.

Worry, which is different from concern over an issue which causes you to take action, is the persistent refusal to do something about something except to allow it to destroy your peace of mind.

One of the defense mechanisms that God gave us for our own protection is legitimate concern. For example, if cancer runs in your family, then follow your doctor's advise regarding diet and medical care. If something appears which you feel is abnormal, that concern should prompt you to see a doctor immediately. Worry, however, is living as though you are doomed by the concern that you refuse to face. Concern over your health may prompt you to get a check-up from your doctor; worry, however, paralyzes you.

May I be very candid and frank? If you are in basic agreement to this point, if you recognize that worry is futile and useless because of God's care and His concern for your life, and yet you worry, call it what it actually is—SIN. "Anyone, then, who knows the good he ought to do and doesn't do it, sins" (James 4:17). And no sin, whether it is socially acceptable like worry is or not, is acceptable in God's sight.

Some people will protest, "But I can't help worrying; it's my nature!" There is no scientific evidence that worry is a part of anyone's nature. Dr. Paul Carlson, a Christian psychiatrist, believes that some individuals are more prone to worry than others by virtue of their emotional and psychological make-up. Just as some have stronger vision than others and some are capable of physical feats far beyond the average, it can only follow that some are more trusting than others and less prone to worry. The vast majority of us choose to worry because we are uncertain that we can really trust God.

To the extent that you can do something about worry, God holds you responsible. Let's face it—you can worry as though there is no God in heaven, or you can determine to trust Him to do what He knows is best. Only He can do that. Maybe you are so close to the problem that you have lost sight of God's magnitude and true greatness. Perhaps, you have never learned the elementary lesson that He is sufficient and powerful enough to handle any situation.

God never intended you to be a prisoner of fear or worry. As Martin Luther once said about temptation, you may not be able to prevent the birds from flying overhead, but you definitely can keep them from building a nest in your hair. The following are some practical guidelines that will help you turn worry into trust.

Guideline One

Acknowledge that worry has become a problem. If there were an organization called Worriers' Anonymous, those who attend the meetings would have to introduce themselves by saying something like, "My name is John Doe, and I'm a worrier!" Admitting that worry has become chronic is the first step toward a long-term solution to the problem.

You may think, "I can handle my problems. Sure, I do a little bit of worrying—everybody does—but I don't need any help." A lot of people cannot handle their problems, and they beat a path to the doors of psychiatrists and counselors. Perhaps you are one of those rugged individualists who can handle them. But, on the other hand, how wise is it for you to carry the burden of worry when God says that you should not? There is a solution by entrusting that concern to Him.

Picture a man walking down the highway with a tremendous pack on his back. He can barely walk under its heavy load as he makes his way slowly toward the city. Then, an empty flat-bed truck comes along. The driver, seeing the weariness of the man, pulls over and says, "Hey, buddy, put your load on my truck bed. I'll take you to town." We'd wonder at the first man's sanity if he said, "No thanks, I can handle my burdens without your help...."

Now, suppose the man with the pack did get up on the back of the empty truck, but he refused to take the pack off, even though he is now riding on the back of the truck. You'd probably doubt his sanity even more, right?

When a believer worries, he is like the man on the flat-bed truck. He could lay his burden down and let the strength of the vehicle move it for him. Christ has paid the price for our burden, and He has indicated His willingness to bear our load if we will entrust it to Him. The first step is to acknowledge that worry has become a problem, and that He is the only one who can do anything about it: "He himself bore our sins [including what worries you] in his body on the tree..." (1 Peter 2:24).

Guideline Two

Ask God in faith to deal with your problem. Remember, Paul's advice? "Don't worry about anything; pray about everything!" Today, we seem to do the reverse: we worry about almost everything and pray about practically nothing. God's psychiatry begins with trust; be specific and ask Him to deal with the problem that kept you turning and tossing last night. Ask Him to come to your aid and remove that nagging thought. Then, take the most difficult step yet.

Guideline Three

Act in obedience to the Word of God in this matter. The Bible says that worries are to be cast upon a Savior who cares. Peter wrote, "Cast all your anxiety on him because he cares for you" (I Peter 5:7). What beautiful words for a world filled with cut-throat competition, a world seemingly so cold and friendless. Psalm 55:22 has similar words of advice: "Cast your cares on the LORD, and he will sustain you."

Guideline Four

Commit to Him what He alone can do. To put God's psychiatry into action requires something fundamental and very difficult: commitment. You need to come to the place where you can say, "I refuse to worry about this. I'm going to turn it over to the Lord and let Him deal with it." So very many of the issues that keep us awake at night, tossing and turning, are things which only God can be responsible for. But our nature is to *fix* things, and when we can't, we worry about it.

A friend of mine tells of an acquaintance who was mountain climbing. The piton—a spike driven into the face of the rock for protection—didn't hold, and he had the sickening sensation that he was going to fall. Sure enough, he fell, and the rope quickly became taut. He only hoped against hope that the piton below that one would hold. He knew that he would certainly fall to his death if it didn't.

Then, after what seemed like eternity, the rope grew taut and held! Though precariously dangling from the end of a rope, he was alive. The measure of the man was that, though his forehead broke out in an icy sweat, he did not panic. He dared not look down, and he kept thinking, "What if that one, lone piton pulls out?" The force of his weight would pull him to his death.

Because he could not look back, he endured several excruciating minutes of agony and worry until his companions reached him. Only when they finally secured him would he allow himself to look below—and he saw that less than three feet beneath him was a ledge wide enough to have easily supported him.

Sometimes we needlessly hang on to our worries, not realizing that underneath are the everlasting arms of God (Deuteronomy 33:27).

Guideline Five

Refuse to worry about your problem again. Once you have committed your worry to the Lord, you've got to make the decision that you are going to leave the problem with Him and not pick up the next morning where you left off the night before. You must refuse to worry, and you can! You can say, "Lord, I turn this need over to You. You work it out, without my help. I refuse to stay awake and be concerned about it. You take over the night shift—no sense in both of us staying awake." You can then turn off the light and say, "Good night, Lord." And then you can have a good night's sleep.

There is one more thing, however, that needs to be said. Once you have taken step five, you aren't finished. There have been times when I had to take that step more than once.

Thinking that I had really committed something to the Lord, I later found myself, usually when I was tired physically, starting to feel concern as I did when I first said, "Lord, I can't handle this—you take it over!"

I heard of a man who was a chronic worrier. If he didn't have legitimate things to worry about, he invented them. If worry had been an Olympic event, surely he would have easily won the gold.

Finally, a friend said, "I know of a wonderful counselor who can help you." Reluctantly, he made an appointment, and he made considerable progress after a few weeks of counseling.

When the two friends met the next time, the chronic worrier seemed happier than he had ever been before.

"It's marvelous what has happened to you!" the friend replied.

"Yes, even though it's costing thousands of dollars, it is worth it."

"But you don't have that kind of money to spend. How will you ever pay the doctor?"

"That's for him to worry about...!"

Discussion Questions:

Joan's grandmother died of cancer, and her mother also died of the serious illness. When Joan develops a lump in her breast, she is overwhelmed with worry. She is convinced that she has the dreaded disease as well, and that even seeing a doctor is futile.

1. In Joan's situation, what would be a healthy concern about this new development? At what point does it become worry and therefore sin? What other response might Joan have to this?

2. Name one thing in your life that causes you to worry. What is the difference between healthy concern about that and sinful worry?

3. What are some ways you can stop the worrying habit?

This will hurt....

It will hurt to keep something that tempts you to worry all to yourself. It will hurt to pretend that that worrisome thing is not present. It will hurt to justify your reasons for worrying.

This will help....

When something causes you concern, stop and think about what you need to do about it. If there is nothing you can do about it, talk to God about what belongs to Him and what is yours.

Try writing down your worry or worries on a piece of paper. Opposite each, note who is responsible for the outcome—*you or God.* For each one that you can do something about, write down what steps you will take to handle the concern. Discipline yourself to get to work on it immediately, even in the face of fear or apathy.

CHAPTER SEVEN

Winning The Inner Struggle Of Fear

There is an Aesop's Fable that pictures Pestilence meeting a caravan on the road to Baghdad.

"Where are you going in such haste?" the leader of the caravan inquires.

"I am going to Baghdad to take 5,000 lives," Pestilence firmly replies. A few days pass, and once more Pestilence and the caravan met.

"You lied! You lied!" the leader of the caravan shouts. "You took not 5,000 lives, but 50,000!"

"No," Pestilence insists, "I took 5,000 and not a soul more. It was Fear who killed all the others."

As we learned in the previous chapter, worry is a destructive habit that robs us of peace of mind. Fear, however, goes much deeper than worry. It is potentially one of the most dangerous of all emotions. "Fears are the most disruptive, destructive things we can have," a medical doctor told me. It is also the first emotion man encountered after creation. When Adam took the forbidden fruit, he lamented his loss of security: "I was afraid" (Genesis 3:10). He knew that he was estranged from God, and that realization brought fear to his heart.

An infant is born with two major fears: the fear of loud noises and the fear of falling. Both relate to a sense of security and well-being. Very quickly, though, the baseline of fear begins to broaden. Each of us has different fears. At different periods in life, we struggle with issues that may appear insignificant to others, but to us they are indeed important.

A childhood fear of the dark, for example, may seem pretty silly to a teenager who, whether or not he admits it, is afraid of rejection by his peer group. That teenager fear isn't so big a deal to his gray-haired grandfather, who fears that he may well run out of money before he dies. My point is that when we wrestle with fear, it is intensely personal and real to the individual who is disturbed by it. It is an inner struggle that the person is going through at a particular time. The depth and intensity of it often cannot be understood by anyone else.

At every point in the journey of life, the things that concern us can create fear. Through my personal experience and through thoughtful observation of human nature, I have noticed that most of our fears revolve around two axes: fear of what we have not personally experienced—something that is not part of our everyday lives; and fear of what might happen, regardless of whether or not there is any real basis for expecting it to happen—such as the fear of being struck by a falling star.

When we are born, every person has three basic needs:

1. The need to give and receive love

2. The need for fulfillment, or the feeling that you are worthwhile to yourself and to other people

3. The need for security.

Fear relates to all of these needs.

The number one fear of children today, school psychologists report, is that Mommy and Daddy may get divorced. That fear is born of the fact that it has happened to so many of their friends. For nearly 50 percent of all grade school children in America, that fear has given way to another one: Does Daddy still love me even though he doesn't live with us anymore? The child knows that Daddy rejected Mommy, and he feels rejected as well, especially when Daddy says repeatedly that he will do something and then doesn't follow through.

Another strong fear for a youngster is that he might be rejected by his peer group. A child wants to be accepted. He doesn't want to stand out from the crowd. Being different may result in rejection by peers who have become a surrogate family when the child doesn't get acceptance at home. Peer pressure can be a positive thing—it may include making A's in school, or going to church on Sunday, or not participating in drugs.

The fear of failure puts a child under pressure as well. Things like the unrealistic expectations of his parents, the inability to measure up to older brothers or sisters, and not *making the team* all create fertile ground for the fear of failure.

Often, though it may not be expressed, the love that children receive comes with strings attached. That is the message that comes through to the child, at least. A child will hear the unexpressed expectations: "If you make us proud of you by making good grades, by keeping your room clean, by behaving yourself, then we will love you!" The greater the emphasis on success, the greater the fear of failure that a child must cope with.

Many of the fears that children have are *caught more than taught*. Their parents and peers have attitudes about or responses to things such as the supernatural, animals, snakes, bats, lizards, death, people of a different race or religion, and a host of other things. The child gets the impression that these are all things to be avoided or feared.

As each of us works through the troubled waters of adolescence and emerges as an adult, we take with us the same framework that was built during childhood. In addition, the differences in sexuality cause men and women to fear different things.

Women are more prone to fear things that would threaten their relationships: Are my children doing okay? Can I balance a job and home responsibilities? Does my husband still see me as attractive, or could I lose him to another woman? Men, on the other hand, are more concerned about their accomplishments: Could I be passed over for promotion? Do my contemporaries respect me? Am I succeeding in my career? Men tend to be goal-oriented, whereas women tend to be relationship-oriented. For both men and women, fear keeps us from getting where we want to be.

Senior adults have fears more focused on health, which includes the fear of death, and the fear of running out of money, which is compounded by inflation, an uncertain economy, and increased longevity.

Just as some people are more prone to worry than others are, some do battle with fear on a far more regular basis. If you are one of those stalwart individuals who fears nothing, count yourself fortunate. Nonetheless, you better not skip this chapter! I've seen people who seemed to fear nothing become absolutely paralyzed in terror when a doctor says, "You have cancer." The big "C" word changed everything.

What Should We Fear?

During World War 2, Franklin Delano Roosevelt encouraged the American people by saying, "There is nothing to fear but fear itself!" Is that necessarily true? I've thought about some of the fears that I've had to face at one time or another. Though I haven't struggled with fear as some do, I freely admit to fearing some things.

I'm not afraid of losing my good looks or the wavy black hair I had in my twenties. The latter departed quite a long while ago, and the former was never an issue. I'm not afraid of death or dying, though I'm certainly not in a hurry for it. I am afraid of rattlesnakes. I am afraid of lightning because I was struck by it once when a bolt of lightning came down the shaft of an umbrella and scorched my thumb. But are these real fears, or are they a healthy appreciation of what could hurt me?

There is something else which I include in my category of fear—God. Surprised? But I'm not afraid of God in the same way that I was afraid of a bully who used to pick on me when I was a kid.

"God is a loving Father," you might say. "Don't you believe that?"

"Certainly," I would reply. "I'm convinced of that."

"Then what are you afraid of?"

Let me illustrate. A Sunday School teacher had a boy in her class who was very "street wise," a tough kid who used his fists more than diplomacy to settle fights. In order to impress him with an idea, she painted a picture of the devil. She intended to put some fear into his heart. After a few minutes she asked, "Now, aren't you afraid of a big devil like that?" He hesitated for a minute and said, "Well, maybe a little bit, but if you'd bring one around my size, I could whip him any time!"

The great and awesome God who simply spoke the word and brought our world into existence, the same God who then breathed life into man, isn't on my level. Therefore, I give Him the respect He deserves.

Twice Scripture says, "The fear of the LORD is the beginning of wisdom" (Psalm 111:10, Proverbs 9:10). At the same time, the New Testament says that perfect love casts out fear (see 1 John 4:18). I know that God loves me, and I have learned to love Him in return. The relationship we have is one of a father and a son. I'm not afraid of God in the way I would be if that relationship did not exist.

But I do reverence Him. Theologians refer to this as a "reverential trust." I understand how great and mighty is our Heavenly Father, but I have no fear of His wrath because I know that, as a child of God, I will never be a target of it.

Understanding The Concern Of God

The greater my understanding of the nature of God and His care and concern for my life, the less will be my fear of many of the issues that paralyze people today. There is a marked relationship between your fears and what you know about God—either correctly or incorrectly. If your concept of God is distorted, possibly because of the image of God you had growing up, what you fear may be irrational. Many people grow up hearing "You'd better be good or God's gonna getcha!" A true understanding of God changes all of that.

As I wrote in my book, *Today Can be Different!,*

What comes to mind as you think about God reveals a great deal about your life; and on the basis of what you tell me about God, I can in all probability tell you a good deal [about your fears]. Your concept of God is to your life what a foundation is to a house, what a periodic chart is to research in a laboratory. It is a fundamental in setting parameters of reality and behavior.[1]

Many people know a great deal about God without really knowing Him. They may commute from the world to the church for an hour a week to enjoy the music and a pep-talk about being a success in life—we used to call this a sermon. They lack a deeper understanding of God, which includes theology, and so they have a smattering of ideas about Him, much like a handful of fine pearls without any string to hold them together to form a necklace.

This is one of the reasons why, in helping someone overcome their fear(s), I always want to know about a person's concept of God.

All Fear Is Not Bad

Adam knew fear because he had broken fellowship with God. The consequences of that took him outside of God's will for His life. At times fear is a marvelous thing. It creates a healthy appreciation of consequences for wrongdoing, and it serves as motivation to safeguard my health, or my family, or what I consider meaningful to me.

I have a healthy appreciation of cancer—but I'm not afraid of it. I've already had my first bout with it, and that was enough to send me to the doctor on a regular basis.

A friend of mine, however, refuses to see a doctor on a regular basis. Her mother died of cancer by the time she was fifty years old, and my friend is too fearful that she may ultimately succumb to the same thing.

In the New Testament, two words are used, both of which are translated as fear. The first group of words relates to the verb stem phobeo. We get our word phobia from that same Greek word. The word generally means *to be afraid* or *to become frightened.* It is also used in regard to people where it means *to show respect* or *to have reverence.*[2]

The second word and its derivatives relate to the Greek word deiliao, which means *to be timid* or *to be cowardly.*[3] It is significant that this is the word Paul used when he said, "For God hath not given us the spirit of fear; but of power, and of love, and of a sound mind" (2 Timothy 1:7, KJV). This kind of fear—or timidity, as other versions translate the word—is the kind that keeps a person from seeing his doctor when he has chest pains. This kind of fear causes people to become prisoners of it, which is contrary to all that God has for you.

How Do We Deal With Irrational Fears?

Telling a child that it is stupid to be afraid of the dark only frustrates the child. What's true is that he is afraid of the dark. If a parent makes light of his fear, the child will also feel shame. When a person is afraid he doesn't have enough money to carry him through old age, you can simply say, "Dad, you've got lots of money, nothing to fear!" But that doesn't bring the same relief as you taking the time to go over his finances, analyze his insurance policies and health care, and project a variety of scenarios to show there is enough money. When an elderly person is afraid of what's going to happen to him, you can say, "You have no need to fear!"Or, you can take your Bible and remind him that God promises to meet all of our needs. The second option brings far more comfort.

When someone is afraid, ridicule, criticism, or minimizing the fear don't work. Logic doesn't always work either, because fear is an emotional response; it is not based on reason.

The following are some guidelines that will help you cope with irrational fears:

Guideline One

Confront your fear. This means getting it out in the open. Talk about it. Admit that it is there. Face it. Sometimes, we expect God to do things for us that He wants us to do. Confronting our fears is one of those.

We are like the little child who repeatedly took the kitchen broom outside to play with it; then, he'd leave it behind when his mother called him for dinner. One evening, his father looked for the broom and could not find it.

"Go outside and get the broom," he said to his son.

"But Daddy, it's dark outside, and I'm afraid."

"Nothing to be frightened of, Son,"his father replied. "God's out there, so go out and get the broom."

Reluctantly, the little boy opened the door. "God, if you are out there, would you please get me the broom!"

God is out there in the dark, but He still expects you to get the broom! You yourself have to confront the fear that is in the dark.

In my book, *Coffee Cup Counseling,* I describe the following scenario:

Your friend Joy misses Bible study for several weeks, and you drop by to see her. As you sit down for a cup of tea together, you let her know that she has been missed. At first she talks about the baby sitter who couldn't take care of the children, but then she bursts into tears and says, "Oh, I might as well tell you what's really bothering me.

I don't know what's gotten into me, but lately whenever I start to back out the car, my hands get cold and sweaty and my heart beats like crazy. I'm scared to death that I'm going to get hit by another car. I don't know what's the matter with me. Dean says I must be losing my mind. Do you think I'm crazy?"[4]

To say to Joy, "It's dumb to be afraid to drive. You've just got to do it," only creates greater apprehension. At times, telling someone what bothers us and what we are afraid of is, in itself, therapy.

It is my belief that every person needs someone in whom he can confide, who will keep his confidence, who will give him the freedom to say whatever is on his mind without passing judgment or rejecting him, to serve as a sounding board. This is what professionals do, yet the responsibility rests on all of us who are part of the family of God.

Guideline Two

Assess the strength of what you fear. Confronting your fear is the first step toward a solution, but confronting it doesn't always eliminate it. The next step is to get a spotlight on it and see how large or small it really is. That is what I mean by assessing the strength of the fear.

Dr. Karl Menninger believed that you can draw a continuum between the ability to cope with life and the inability to cope with it—between sanity and insanity, if you will. But on this continuum, there is no clearly defined place at which you have moved from one side to the other. Every person goes through periods in life when he or she is better able to do battle with his or her inner struggles, and that includes fear.

So, is it necessary to eliminate or directly deal with everything you fear? As surprising as it may seem, my answer is "NO!" Some things just don't matter. Let me illustrate.

I thought I knew my wife pretty well before we married, but six months into our marriage we were in Paris, doing some of the usual *tourist* things. To save money, we decided to take the elevator up the Eiffel tower and walk down. Fine! What we didn't know, at the time, is that the staircase is exterior, which means that it winds back and forth down the outside of the tower.

We had gone only a short way when I learned something new about my wife: Darlene is afraid of heights—*acrophobia*. She does fine when she is close to the ground, but get her close to the edge of anything with a sheer drop and she freezes. The same thing happened when we tried skiing. When she froze, I said, "It's O.K., Honey. You don't have to ski downhill." We switched to cross country skiing, and everybody is happy. Not all fears have to be overcome.

Guideline Three

Deal with the fear you can do something about. Some fears you need to confront, like fears about your health, and some fears can be accommodated. But what about the person whose fear inhibits his or her life? Some people have jobs that require travel, yet they are afraid of flying on airplanes? What about the woman who has a job as a sales representative? Should she sweat and bear it? Have her stomach knot even just thinking about it? I've sat next to individuals on the airplane who were afraid to fly. Some think that the only way to beat the fear of flying is to drown it, and I usually learn about the person's fear after his second drink.

At times, counseling helps eliminate the problem by getting the fear out in the open and talking about it. Even with the fear of flying, therapy groups have successfully helped people overcome the fear by giving them exposure to the mechanics of planes and flying.

Some people have had inordinate fears about computers or telephone recorders, and they have, through experience, come to learn that these are simply mechanical devices that do what they are told to do. A computer will not reach out and bite the hand that feeds it a floppy disk, and an answering machine cannot read your mind.

The fear of death has been described as man's greatest fear. Who would deny that any unexpected encounter with death creates fear? Most of us can appreciate Mark Twain's comment that he wished he knew where he was going to die, because if he did, he would never go near the place.

When a doctor says, "If you know how to pray, you had better do so because medical science has nothing to offer," we are gripped with cold fear. In reality, every person on Planet Earth is terminal. The fact is that you will die, eventually. I have seen a person who had a "terminal" illness outlive half a dozen of his friends who had normal life expectancies. The genealogies in the book of Genesis show the ongoing litany of a father who begot a son and died; then, the son became a father who gave birth to his son, and he died. We need to remember that matters of life and death are in God's hands.

J. C. Penney cut man's greatest fear down to size. At the height of the Great Depression, Penney was losing everything he had worked so hard for. He ended up in the hospital with ulcers that threatened his life. His diet was milk and crackers. His nerves were on edge. And he was very much afraid that he was dying.

While he lay in bed, he heard the words of a song drift down the corridors of the hospital, "Be not dismayed what e'er betide; God will take care of you." Those words sunk into his heart, and, according to Penny's own testimony, they turned his life around. His fear vanished and his faith in God's watch-care grew.

The Bible contends that life and death are not a matter of indifference to our Heavenly Father. He has numbered the very hairs of your head and knows when each sparrow falls to the ground? This, of course, must be taken by faith, and faith is what puts fear to flight.

Believing that God is a good God and that He cares about you is a powerful antidote to the venom of fear. This was the confident assurance of the Psalmist, King David. He recalled how, as a lad, he would take his father's sheep through the valley between Bethlehem and Jericho. That passage was known as the "valley of the shadow of death," because it often claimed the lives of shepherds when the rain from cloudbursts swiftly ran down the barren hillsides and drowned the shepherd with his sheep.

We can say with David, "The Lord is my shepherd.... Even though I walk through the valley of the shadow of death, I will fear no evil, for you are with me; your rod and your staff, they comfort me" (Psalm 23:1,4).

Dr. Jack Morris, a pastor and psychotherapist, often asks his patients who are struggling with fear to memorize Psalm 23 and recite it out loud several times a day. "...God has said, 'Never will I leave you; never will I forsake you.' So we say with confidence, 'The Lord is my helper; I will not be afraid. What can man do to me?" (Hebrews 13:5).

It is no wonder that David cried out, "The LORD is my light and my salvation—whom shall I fear? The LORD is the stronghold of my life—of whom shall I be afraid?" (Psalm 27:1). The assurance that God is with us, that His actual presence surrounds us, that nothing can happen to us apart from His will, cuts life's greatest fears down to size (see Isaiah 43:1-3).

Guideline Four

Commit to the Lord what you cannot change or understand. A computer Bible concordance will quickly make up a list of 365 "fear nots" in the Bible—one for every day of the year. Some fears still hang around, even when we confess, confront, and find comfort in the promises of Scripture. These are fears we must commit to our Heavenly Father daily.

As long as we are alive, there will be situations that create fear. "For when we came into Macedonia," Paul wrote to the Corinthians, "this body of ours had no rest, but we were harassed at every turn—conflicts on the outside, fears within. But God, who comforts the downcast, comforted us..." (2 Corinthians 7:5,6).

I have known the cold, gnawing feeling of fear in the pit of my stomach, but I have also heard the voice of the Shepherd and have felt the comfort of His presence. And so can you. You can win over the inner struggle of fear through faith. It works!

Discussion Questions:

Robert and Steven were rock climbing when one of the pitons pulled out. Robert plummeted through the air almost forty feet before Steven was able to stop his fall. For a time, Robert was frozen in panic, and Steven helped him overcome the fear so that Robert had the confidence to continue with the climb.

1. What are some of the thoughts that might be going through Robert's mind that keep him frozen in fear? If you were Steven, how would you help Robert keep climbing?

2. What is one concern in your life that has turned into fear? Try to set aside the paralyzing feelings for a moment: when you think about the circumstances objectively, do they warrant that amount of fear? What are some things that set you up for letting a legitimate concern turn into fear that freezes you in action. These might be past experiences, watching someone else go through something similar, etc.?

3. Describe, in your own words, God's tender care for you. How might realizing that help you put this particular fear in perspective?

4. What is one fear in your life that you do not need to confront or overcome? What are your reasons for deciding to not work on eliminating that? What can you do instead of confronting that fear?

This will hurt....

Sometimes, when someone else has a fear that is not real for you, you might be tempted to dismiss it as silly or not important. It does no good to tell the person that there is nothing to worry about, or to remind him of the good things in life. Fear, whatever the source, is very real to the person who is feeling it. It will hurt to remind the person that *there is nothing to fear but fear itself.*

This will help....

Some fears are never eliminated entirely, but they can be overcome so that you do not live frozen by their influence. It will help to reassure the person that fear is normal, and that we all have different fears. Be a sounding board for someone who is afraid, and suspend judgment about their feelings. The age-old advice of putting yourself in another person's shoes is good advice. Imagine yourself with his background and his situation, and try to understand his fears instead of dismissing them.

Notes

[1] Harold J. Sala, *Today Can Be Different,* (Ventura California: Regal Books, 1988), July 17 selection.

[2] F. Wilbur Gingrich, *Lexicon of the Greek New Testament,* (Chicago: The University of Chicago Press, 1965), p. 230.

[3] Ibid. p. 46.

[4] Harold J. Sala, *Coffee Cup Counseling,* (Nashville: Thomas Nelson Publishers, 1989), p. 146.

CHAPTER EIGHT

The Name Of The Malady Is Boredom

In her book, *The Feminine Mystique,* Betty Friedman has a chapter entitled, "The Problem That Has No Name." She discusses the plight of a growing number of women around the world who are bored, dissatisfied with life, and thoroughly unhappy. Such was the feeling of a twenty-year-old mother who put it in these words:

> "I ask myself why I am so dissatisfied. I've got my health, fine children, a lovely new home, enough money. My husband has a real future as an electronics engineer. He doesn't have any of these feelings. He says maybe I need a vacation, but that isn't it! I can't sit down and read a book alone. If the children are napping, I just walk through the house waiting for them to wake up. Then you wake up one morning, and there's nothing to look forward to!"

Harry Johnson, a medical doctor writing for Reader's Digest, said:

> Today's civilization, the most advanced in history, with the highest standard of living ever known, has produced a generation of bored, apathetic people. We seek entertainment, yet find it dull—even a great performance in the theater is often rewarded by hoards of people leaving before the curtain falls. We sit in front of TV sets watching a succession of plays, shows, and movies without really noticing what we are seeing. We leaf aimlessly through newspapers and magazines. When we say, "I'm tired," many of us really mean, "I'm tired of what I'm doing. I'm tired of my way of life."[1]

The problem that Betty Friedman says has no name is often described as boredom. It's a problem shared by people from all classes and all ranks. What you have or what you don't have is no guarantee that you can't fall prey to this insidious thing, and become its victim. Rich and poor, gifted and neglected, intellectuals and those who are somewhat dull, are all found in the ranks of the bored.

The problem is not peculiar to women. Men, as often as women, get bored and indifferent with life. A businessman went to his doctor complaining of feeling bad, though he couldn't pinpoint the trouble. The doctor ordered laboratory tests and gave the man a thorough examination, but they didn't turn up any real physical problem. The man came back for further consultation. After a few words of pleasantries, the doctor turned to him and said, "I have good news for you. The physical exam hasn't turned up a single problem whatsoever. I can give you a clean bill of health."

Instead of being elated, the man complained, "Doctor, I am tired from the minute I get up in the morning until I go to bed at night." The doctor wisely recognized the man's problem as not physical in nature. He saw that the problem was boredom, and he began pointing out all the advantages in life that had come to this man—a good business, a nice home, almost everything money could buy, as well as an attractive wife, and children. Bluntly, the man responded, "They can have it; I'm bored stiff with it."

Boredom is not only one of the major causes of fatigue—that listless feeling that leaves you constantly tired out—but it is also one of the factors contributing to broken homes. It is one of the reasons that both men and women walk out the door and never come back.

The Relationship Of Boredom To Fatigue

Let's talk about the relationship between boredom and fatigue. For a moment, think with me about your own life—the day that you had last week when nothing seemed to go right, the day you were constantly interrupted. Perhaps, it wasn't last week; maybe it was yesterday. Or maybe it was a whole week of days that seem to blur together.

Every time you started to get to your work, something happened. The phone rang. Somebody dropped by for a friendly chat. You would like to have said, "Friend, I'd like to sit and talk for a while, but I don't have the time." But you were afraid of offending him, so you sat and killed more time. Each time you got started with your work, you were interrupted again, and again, and again. All the time, you had the burden of your work hanging over your head. At the end of the day, you reviewed your accomplishments, which were zero-minus. You really didn't do anything, but you went home tired out—from the work? NO! From the tension that produced the weariness.

Then, the next day, maybe everything clicked. You got started and your work fell together. That night when you went home, you felt great. Actually, you put out a lot more energy than you did when you were so frustrated, but the difference is that accomplishment defeated fatigue. When people begin to lose interest in their lives, feeling that it is a squirrel-cage existence—the same thing day after day after day—they begin to suffer from weariness. Weariness is a gnawing tiredness that can't be defeated by vitamins or pills.

When Dr. Edward Thorndike of Columbia University conducted a series of experiments relating boredom to fatigue, he kept a group of students awake for almost a week by constantly changing their interests. Dr. Thorndike concluded his tests with the following statement: "Boredom is the only real cause of fatigue."[2] Don't think for a moment that if you are sufficiently interested in what you do that you can give up a getting a good night's sleep on a regular basis. But if you recognize that part of your weariness is really caused by boredom, you can follow the prescription for its cure and get a new grip on life.

Boredom not only takes its toll in our bodies physically, it takes its toll on our marriages and our homes as well. When a couple begins to take each other for granted and their relationship loses the freshness and sparkle that it once had, boredom begins to set in.

Statistically, there are three dangerous periods in marriage. The first period, as you might suspect, is during the first couple of years when a couple really begins to know each other. The problems during this period are caused by the couple adjusting to each other, not by boredom. The second critical period is after a couple has been married for seven to ten years, when they have settled down into a routine. By then they usually have children and a mortgage on the house. Unless they keep their love alive, they begin to think, "Is this all there is to life?"

The third period of stress comes when a couple has been married for twenty to twenty-five years. The children are grown, and the man and woman are over the age of forty and facing the physical and emotional changes of middle age. By this time, he is struggling with the 3-b's: bulges, balding, and bifocals. She no longer looks good in a two-piece swimsuit at the beach. Both have aged, and both sometimes wonder if they still have what it takes to attract members of the opposite sex.

Though men are more prone to want to prove to themselves that they are still able to charm someone else, both men and women can become bored with their mates—wrong as that is. There is no more reason for a husband and a wife to allow themselves to grow bored with each other than there is to grow bored with potatoes or rice.

In marriage, the deadly virus of boredom can infect us in many ways. It infects us when we allow ourselves to take each other for granted, when we begin to presume upon each other, when we lose the freshness and sparkle of romance in a relationship. The process of courtship or dating serves as a time when a couple can really get to know each other. But it also serves to meet an important need that we have all our lives called *companionship.*

The quiet evenings when you strolled through the park or by the beach in the moonlight served to meet emotional needs for both the man and the woman. But, in some cases, when a man crosses the threshold of marriage, he allows himself to think, "I've won the battle—I've got her. She is my wife now." He no longer sees any need to take his wife out, open her car door, or spend an evening together in a little restaurant that used to be their favorite haunt.

Boredom sets in when a couple begins to lose touch with each other. Communication is a mutual exchange of thoughts, ideas, information, and emotions between two people. When a couple has been married for a dozen years or so, they sometimes stop talking. They think they have said everything there is to say, and so they bury their thoughts in the television set or hide behind a newspaper. They grow further apart and more bored with each other. The problem is not that people grow tired of marriage; they grow tired of each other because they haven't kept their relationship alive. Though she knows it is wrong, a woman finds herself being influenced when, bored with her husband, she meets another person who seems to have the personality and zest for life that has long since been lost in her husband.

There is another aspect to the problem of boredom, and that has to do with the intertwining of the spiritual with every phase of our lives. Boredom comes to us when we begin to lose touch with God, and this often happens at the same time we begin to lose touch with a spouse. You can't compartmentalize your life, calling one area physical, another emotional, and a third spiritual. When the level of excitement begins to drop in life, it sinks in all three areas. That is why an emotional problem—*boredom*—results in a physical problem—*fatigue*, and we often see spiritual back-sliding at the same time.

So what are some things that can help you with this?

Guideline One

Overcome boredom by discovering God's will for your life. Let's go back to some simple fundamentals for a moment. That God should have a will for your life should be no harder for you to accept than the fact there is order and precision in nature itself. The planets are kept in their orbits by the precise relationship to other bodies. We call that the Law of Gravitation. The 23.5° tilt of the earth on its axis is responsible for producing the seasons. And the intricate composition of molecules gives order to life itself.

Now, if God has a will for these things, it should not be difficult to realize that God also has a will for you. It begins when you come to Christ and receive Him as your personal Savior. In Ephesians chapter five we are told that we are not to be ignorant, but we need to understand what the will of God really is. At another time, I'll deal with the subject of how to find the will of God, but for right now, suffice it to say that God has one for your life.

It could very well be that your boredom is caused from a lack of God-direction in your life. You have no purpose, no goal, and you are uncertain of yourself and your destiny. You are cut off from God and you wander aimlessly from one thing to another, searching and seeking but tired of it all. The result is boredom and fatigue. You are like an airplane pilot in a storm, searching for a landing field, but unable to see anything at all.

In the pages of the Bible, we read of men and women whose lives were so very human. But whatever other difficulties they faced, their problem was never boredom. A spiritual purpose in life eliminates the boredom that comes to so many. With no sense of identity, no realization of why they are here, no goal of eternal destiny, people wander from one tasteless thrill to another, searching, seeking, but never quite finding. They never come to a knowledge of the truth.

In the biographies of outstanding Christian leaders—Martin Luther, John Wesley, John Calvin, Dwight L. Moody, George Mueller, R. A. Torrey, and a host of others—you will discover that there were times when they were weary and tired from physical exhaustion, but they were seldom "bored" and without a sense of purpose in life.

Contrast that sense of purpose that they have in common with the lives today of so many bored and apathetic individuals, people who are so indifferent to life itself. Many people today have an abundance of material possessions, yet they are faced with spiritual poverty.

A spiritual purpose in life eliminates the emptiness and weariness that drives men and women to the brink. If your boredom is because you have no spiritual purpose in your life, do something about it. Invite Jesus Christ to be your Lord and Savior. If you have already taken this step, get back into the center of God's will. The very realization that God has a will for you gives life a sense of purpose. There is an ultimate destiny to life, and yours can cease to be an endless wandering.

Suppose you've taken that first step. Where do you go from there?

Guideline Two

Overcome boredom by realistically setting some goals for your life and home. Recently, a business analyst reproved business men, charging that men set goals and have aspirations for their businesses, but that, when it comes to their families and personal lives, they have no plans or goals for the future at all. He charged that a lot of men don't know why they married their wives, and they do not know what they want out of life. And he is right!

Goals for a family have to be a great deal more than just material. They must also include qualities that you want to see in the lives of your children, and a plan as to how you can help them become the kind of young men and women you would like to see them become. Goals may include educational objectives for them and you, as well as cultural and spiritual objectives.

The goals of life have to be flexible, however; when they are not flexible and they become unobtainable, we tend to give up and grow bored.

A young man went to his physician, who happened to be a Christian, and said, "Everything seems to be such an effort;

I'm chronically tired." There did not seem to be a physical problem, and as the young man poured out his heart, the problem became more clear. The young man said that he had always wanted to become a doctor, but he had played around in school and his poor grades had kept him out of medical school. The result was a young man who was frustrated and perfectly miserable in his job—constantly tired out and bored with life.

The doctor wisely advised the young man to realign his goals and purposes in life, and start moving toward them. What about you? When you fail, do you drag through life bored and defeated by this failure complex, or do you set new goals and begin to move toward them?

If you remain in your little castle of gloom, boredom sets in. You can break out of it, however, with new objectives and new goals that are pleasing to the Lord. Sam, a mechanic, did just that. He had one of the dullest jobs in his company. Every day he stood at a lathe and turned out bolts. He dreaded waking up each morning to face another endless day of standing in the same spot and doing the same thing over again. He wanted to quit, but jobs were hard to come by. He was afraid that if he quit, he wouldn't be able to find another job. In the meanwhile, he had a wife and kids to feed.

He felt locked in, but since he couldn't quit, he thought of new goals, new ways that he could make a dull job more interesting.

"I've got it!" he thought. "A little competition with the other lathe operators." He began competing with some of the other men, just to break the boredom of doing the same thing every day. What happened? His work started improving. Not only was the speed impressive, but the quality of the work also improved. That was the beginning of a series of promotions that eventually led Mr. Samuel Vauclain to the presidency of the Baldwin Locomotive Works.

Is your job as boring as the one Sam had? Then what can you do to make it more interesting? Sometimes, we are not so bored with our work as we are bored with ourselves. We keep looking for a new thrill, a new jolt, something for kicks, thinking that the problem is the environment—everybody else—when the real problem is with ourselves. Remember the comic strip character by the name of Pogo whom I described in the forword of this book? His one-liner is right on target: "We have met the enemy, and he is us!"

When the problem is with you, a change of jobs will only produce temporary relief from the boredom. Eventually, your new job will grow boring and stale as well.

Guideline Three

Overcome boredom by injecting enthusiasm into your work by doing everything *as unto the Lord.* Here's the familiar Word to back it up: "Whatever you do, work at it with all your heart, as working for the Lord, not for men" (Colossians 3:23). Paul had just given instructions to husbands, to wives, to children, and also to slaves, and he summarizes all of it with that advice. What he is really saying is, "Man, get with it! Don't go dragging through life. Whatever you do, do it with all your heart as though you were doing it specifically for the Lord, and not for some other reason!" Once you grasp this simple thought—or better yet, let this tremendous thought grasp you—you will never be the same person. This concept puts enthusiasm in the dullest job. It lifts it right out of a boring setting and makes it come alive.

Paul wasn't the first person to sense this guidance from the Lord. A thousand years before, the writer of Ecclesiastes said, "Whatever your hand finds to do, do it with all your might, for in the grave, where you are going, there is neither working nor planning nor knowledge nor wisdom" (Ecclesiastes 9:10).

Here's what an impact this can have. Several years ago, a charming, refined college professor came to me with a problem. She was one of the most gracious persons I had ever met. She had never married, and she had given herself totally to her work, gaining considerable prestige as the author of several mathematics textbooks that had a very wide circulation. Frankly, I was a little surprised to hear her unburden her heart.

She said, "I have a problem and I need help with it. I'm a terrible housekeeper and I know that it is not right, but I don't know what to do about it." Her life had been the classroom, and by the time she got home, she just wasn't interested in the proper end of a broom. Over many years, the magazines and books, along with her personal effects, had literally overflowed the closets and were stacked to the ceiling. We talked about the concept given to us in the words of Scripture, and that we can face unpleasant tasks in life if we realize that we are not doing it for any reason other than for the Lord.

What happened? Did it go in one ear and out the other? Not on your life! The first thing she did was to put a couple of college boys to work carting enough things out of the house to stock a thrift store. Boxes and boxes of discarded magazines and students' papers went to the dump. Gradually, the floors and closets began to reappear. She began to scrub and to scour, and her housework became not only bearable but likable.

The story I've shared with you won't be found in the introduction to the mathematics textbooks she has written, but believe me, it is the story of a life gripped with the concept that the most boring task can come alive if you take God into it.

My second illustration is about a woman who was known as "Teacher" to thousands of men and women. Among the most gifted and unusual persons I've ever met was Henrietta

Mears, a great Christian educator. She was responsible for the establishment of Gospel Light Press, one of the great Christian printing firms. She was also the inspiration behind the founding of Forest Home Christian Conference Center in California. She was a major influence in the life of Dr. Bill Bright, founder of Campus Crusade, and a woman who majored in *enthusiasm*. In fact, her friends referred to her as "Public Energy Number One."

I'll never forget the afternoon I met her for the first time. I had just finished my master's degree and I had a couple of weeks free. She had agreed to let me follow in her shadow for that time so I could see what made her tick.

It didn't take long. Ethel Baldwin, her secretary, introduced me as I came into her simple, yet tasteful office. With no ado, Dr. Mears briskly snapped, "Sit down, young man. In the next two hours, you're going to learn more about Christian education than you did all the time you were in school!" Like a machine gun firing with enthusiasm, she was off and running! That afternoon, I did learn something that isn't terribly academic in nature but it is more important than anything the academic may produce: if you don't have enthusiasm, you will never get yourself or your message across.

In the economy of God, there is no such thing as an unimportant task. The wife and mother who faces a sink full of dirty dishes and a basket of little clothes that must be sorted is helping to build a cathedral made up of people. God is the architect of this great cathedral called the home, and she is helping to shape the destiny of lives. God has endowed the commonplace with virtue and meaning for those who know Him.

Guideline Four

Search out the needs of others, and give some of your time and talent to help someone less fortunate than you. Nobody in the company is quite as bored as the one who has only selfish interests in working there.

Whenever Lillian Dickson, whose story has been featured by Readers' Digest, spoke in the church I pastored, we always had to find something she could stand on. Her diminutive stature just wouldn't let her see over the top of the pulpit. But dynamite, as they say, comes in small packages!

When her missionary husband died in Taiwan, everyone expected her to pack up and go home like most widows would have done. But not Lil Dickson. Instead of resigning herself to a life of boredom and ease, she rolled up her sleeves and accomplished far more than she ever did as the wife of a missionary and seminary professor.

Her efforts led to hospitals for the needy of Taiwan, clinics for leprosy patients, orphanages, homes for unwed mothers, and training centers for orphans and delinquent children. This remarkable woman traveled over rugged mountains, establishing churches in primitive areas. Even when she was beyond the age at which most people retire, Lillian Dickson was full of life and energy. That word, boredom, was never part of her vocabulary. She was involved with the needs of others.

Apart from her dynamic outlook and "can do" approach to problem solving, another thing that impressed me about this great woman is that she never wasted time on "small talk." And she lacked the patience necessary to have clothes tailored for her, which was the way it was done in Taiwan then. Instead, she had every dress made just the same from one pattern. Boring? Not to her! What counted to her was different from what counts to most people.

What about you? Have you learned that, from God's perspective, the small task in front of you is just as important as the big, glamorous one? Very few days are like the brilliance of a Roman candle. Life is filled with the commonplace and the mundane.

If you can sense the fact that there is a spiritual purpose in changing the linens on the beds or standing at the lathe and grinding out the same thing day after day after day, boredom will give way to meaning and purpose. Sometimes, we are so close to the tasks of life that we just don't see the overall purpose in them. As the expression goes, "We are too close to the forest to see the trees."

A Postscript On Boredom

Finding the cause of your boredom and isolating the problem allows you to step back far enough to get the perspective you need to deal with it. Masking the problem, which does have a name after all, or trying to escape it in some way isn't sufficient. It must be dealt with, and you can do that with God's help. Failing to deal with any problem compounds your inner struggles, and it contributes to another enormous problem—stress. I'll discuss that in the next chapter.

Discussion Questions:

Betty has worked as a receptionist for the same real estate company for eight years. Every day, she keeps a fresh pot of coffee brewing, and shuffles paper in between answering the phone. Every night, when she gets home from the office, she complains to her daughter that her job is boring.

1. How might the boredom affect how Betty feels about herself and her role at the office? What can she do to make that job more interesting, provided she wants to keep it?

2. Think of a time in your life when you were bored for an extended period of time. What affect did that have on your energy level and your relationships? What steps did you take to get past that period—either to make the situation more interesting or to get out of the situation? Was there any permanent negative impact on your life or your relationships?

3. Name two things that you feel are a waste of your time, insignificant but necessary responsibilities. What are three positive and important affects each of those have in your life or someone else's?

4. Get a piece of paper and divide it into three columns. Label one column **My Job**, another **My Relationship(s)**, and the third **My Fun**. Write down three goals under each heading, no matter how basic or grand those goals might be, leaving space between each goal. Next, think through and write down what it will take to make those goals a reality. Then—and this is the hard part!—get to work on those steps!

This will hurt...

If you are bored, it will hurt to sit still and wallow in your boredom. God meant for our lives to be vital and productive. It will hurt to dwell on the negative aspects of the situation, and it will hurt to convince yourself that nothing will ever change.

This will help...

A Peanuts cartoon summed it up well when someone said, "We are overwhelmed with insurmountable opportunities!" If you are bored at work, start looking for things that need to be done or ways that the situation can be improved. You might want to share your ideas with your boss. If you are bored in a friendship, talk with the other person about how you can bring the fun back in. If you are bored with yourself, take a class, start a new hobby, or do something you've always wanted to do.

Turning boredom into challenge will help move you forward personally, professionally, or relationally.

Notes

[1]Harry Johnson, "That Tired Feeling—Its Cause and Cure," Readers Digest, Oct., 1966, pp 142-143.

CHAPTER NINE

Coping With Stress

When was the last time you reached for the bottle of aspirin and washed a couple down with a glass of water? When was the last time you had an afternoon of leisure, with no agenda apart from what you wanted to do—maybe a quiet walk on the beach or a stroll through the woods where you could drink in the smells of damp leaves and moss and enjoy the beautiful wild flowers? Which of those two times was easier for you to remember? Most of us can recall headaches much faster than walks in nature.

The tension headache that made you snarl at your kids, grouch at your mate, and want to kick the cat didn't mean you had a brain tumor or needed to see a neurologist. Nonetheless, it was a red flag. Your nervous system screamed, "Help! I'm overloaded; I just can't handle this!"

You're not alone. Tension headaches regularly trouble as many as 100 million Americans every year. These 100 million Americans go to doctors who write 200 million prescriptions for tons of pain killers.

The name of this problem is stress, "a state of physical and emotional arousal caused by demands, pressures, and the wear and care of life." But you know what it is!

Stress is what you feel when...

- Your teenage daughter says, "Dad, you know that guy I met from Zambia? Well, we're going to elope!"
- There is too much month at the end of your money.
- You are late for a flight and learn that the next plane arrives after the wedding.
- You look in the rear view mirror and see a red light flashing.
- Your husband gets passed over for promotion.
- Your rich aunt finally dies and you've been cut out of the will.
- It's the week before Thanksgiving, and you are the turkey!

Stress shows itself in different ways to different people:

- The businessman who tries to make a profit in a down market feels the effects of stress.
- The salesman who tries to reach his quota and earn the big bonus, but who finds his goal always seems to be just a step ahead of him knows what stress is.
- The single parent who has to be cook, bottle-washer, chauffeur, both mom and dad, all while trying to keep his or her own act together can identify stress.

- The college student who faces the keen pressure of competition knows stress.

- The medical professional on the graveyard shift who tries to meet the needs of patients single-handedly because half the staff didn't even bother to call in sick understands stress.

Let's personalize it. Finish this sentence:

Stress is what I feel when _____.

Take a few minutes and evaluate your stress level.

Dr. Hans Seyle has been conducting research on stress since 1936. Having written more than 33 books and 1600 articles on the subject, I think it is safe to say that this Canadian-born endocrinologist has done more work on the subject than any man alive! Seyle doesn't believe that we are facing more stress today than our parents and grandparents did. What he does believe is that we are not handling it as well.

However, if the letters that come to our office each week as the result of our more than 2500 radio broadcasts are any barometer of what is happening to us, I believe that we are facing stress in quantities Grandfather never imagined in his worst nightmare. Researchers tell us that stress is doing everything from producing cancer to lowering the IQ of our children.

All Stress Is Not Bad

It is stress that causes the tension that holds a suspension bridge over raging waters. Stress on the strings of the violin allows the beautiful melody to come from the fingers of the master as the bow glides across the strings. Stress on the drum head allows the instrument to resonate as the drummer beats it.

But too much stress causes the suspension bridge to collapse, the string of the violin to snap, and the drum head to burst.

Some folks actually thrive on stress.

The goalie in the world cup goes out on the field knowing that success or failure may depend on his stopping that ball from hitting the net. Yet not his mother, the Apostle Paul, or an angel from heaven would be able to stop him from going out there. He's going to go for it!

A lot of folks actually do perform better, sell more convincingly, or rise to greater levels of accomplishment when they are under a certain amount of stress.

No matter who you are, though, too much stress can kill you!

What Excessive Stress Does

When you are confronted with a stressful situation, it takes only fifteen seconds for the hypothalamus gland in your brain to trigger the burst of adrenaline that begins to surge through your veins. This causes what psychologists describe as the "fight or flight" syndrome.

1. Stress affects your emotions. A rainbow of emotional responses, from anger to fear, may be triggered when you are under prolonged stress, and emotional responses that are normally pretty cool and measured become strained. You become irritable and cross, and you probably say things you really don't mean. It is usually members of your family who become the victims of your stress.

Most family arguments take place within thirty minutes of the dinner hour. This is usually when at least one person has come home under stress and reacts in a way he or she couldn't on the job. Stress can produce in a person *the disposition of a junk yard dog,* a dog that is cruising for a fight.

2. Stress affects your body. Double your fist up for a full minute as you read the rest of this page. Before you even finish reading you'll notice that your fist begins to throb. God didn't intend for you to walk around with your hand tensed like a lethal weapon. But when you are under stress, your stomach begins to knot just like your fist. You can't tell your stomach, "Hey, stomach, just relax!" so you have your "Maalox moment" as you try to calm your nerves.

Tension headaches account for 80 percent of the symptoms that bring people to their doctor. Jane Broady, in the New York Times Guide to Personal Health, says:

When most people talk about stress, they mean the negative reactions: a churning gut, aching back, tight throat, rapid heartbeat, elevated blood pressure, mental depression, short temper, crying jags, insomnia, impotence, viral infections, asthma attacks, ulcers, heart disease, or cancer.

Those are definitely physical problems that will drive a person to a doctor.

3. Stress affects your spiritual life. When you are under stress you feel like you are doing something wrong. God seems distant and remote. Then, you also feel guilty because you feel the way you do. This gives rise to two myths, two misconceptions, that can haunt you:

Myth One
Christians shouldn't face stress.

Myth Two
Those who do are not spiritual!

The editor of a Christian magazine heard me quote John Powell in one of my radio programs on the subject of stress: "When you repress your emotions, your stomach keeps score."

Later, she wrote:

This was your voice followed in a brief minute by your praying for strength for those struggling with this problem. To which I replied, "Praise the Lord" and cried. Yesterday I was told by my physician that there is a strong possibility that I have an ulcer. I must go in Monday for tests to try and determine this or discover what other possibility it might be. This sets hard with me as in my opinion, ulcers and Christians should not go together. I equate this with a lack of dependence on God.

If you feel like this friend does, ponder this for a minute: In your living room is an end table which was designed to support a lamp, a vase, and maybe a few trinkets or magazines. It handles the weight adequately when it is used the way it was designed to be used. Now, suppose you need to put up new drapes. You hate to bother with getting the ladder out of the garage. You take a good look at the table and think, "I can stand on that!" and you pull it over to the window.

It wobbles a bit, but it holds your weight. However, you can't quite reach the top of the drapes, so you call your husband, who is watching TV, and he comes to your assistance. If both of you stand on that table, it will probably collapse under the weight.

So the table collapsed because it was not a spiritual table, right?

Wrong!

Spirituality has nothing to do with the issue of stress. The table didn't come from the drawing board of the designer to be used as a ladder. By using it in that way, you violated the purpose for which it was created. In the same way, there are load limits to what each of us can handle. When we carry greater burdens that our Designer intended us to, spirituality is not the primary issue: load limit is.

To think that believers in Jesus Christ shouldn't face the consequences of stress is about as realistic as saying that Christians should never have colds or the flu. But at the same time, the way you as a Christian view stressful circumstances has a great deal to do with how well you cope with them.

Actually, there can be situations when a person's stress level is appreciably increased because of his faith. Take, for example, the woman who wants to take her children to church on Sunday morning when her husband wants her to stay home, prepare breakfast and keep him company. Her going to church might make him feel guilty, which will only increase his irritability and, in turn, create higher stress levels.

Also, scores of people can readily testify to the fact that fellow employees know of their faith, and, because they do not share the same viewpoint, make negative comments that create stress between them.

God's People Have Always Known Stress

Daniel sits in the lion's den. He knows that if his prayers don't reach heaven fast, he's on the menu for breakfast. That's terminal stress, as I see it.

Remember Esther? She is convinced that the only way she can save the Jewish people, her people, is to risk her life by going before the king without being called. "If I perish, I perish!" she cries. That's stress any way you define it.

Consider the stress Joseph faced. After being sold into slavery by his own brothers, he was eventually falsely accused of sexual assault, wrongly convicted, and thrown into prison. Most men would have succumbed to the advances of Potiphar's wife, and Joseph might have thought, "God, is this what I get for playing it straight?" There is no record that he felt *put upon* by the Almighty, but you can be sure that he felt stress. Any person who has known the despair of hearing the key turn in the jail door can testify to that!

Elijah knew stress as he watched the waters in the brook Kerith dry up. Maybe you have seen your finances do that same thing.

Anyone who has ever taken a tour group to Israel and tried to satisfy the whims of an entire group knows—in a very, very small way—the stress that Moses experienced as He tried to keep 2.5 million people satisfied in the desert.

David knew stress. Anointed by Samuel to be king, David watched months turned into years as he waited. He became a fugitive from the angry fits of King Saul, who didn't want to relinquish his throne. For seven long years David fled for his life, finally casting his lot with the Philistines, the enemies of Israel.

If there had been Olympic gold medals given for stress, surely Paul would have won one. Take, for example, the stress he experienced on his second missionary journey. It began when Paul had an argument with his best friend, Barnabas.

Barnabas: "Let's take John Mark on this trip!"

Paul: "No way, Barney! Remember, he chickened out and quit on us on the last trip!"

Barnabas: "If he doesn't go, I don't go!"

And he didn't!

That was stressful!

So Paul took Silas and they journeyed to Troas, where he planned on turning east into Bythinia (modern Russia), but God closed the door. Anyone who has had a trip interrupted by delays or visa rejection knows the stress it creates.

Paul turned west and he and Silas ended up in a prison in Philippi, with their feet in stocks and their backs burning from the stripes which were unjustly laid on them. Yet Paul could write to the Corinthians: "We are hard pressed on every side, but not crushed; perplexed, but not in despair; persecuted, but not abandoned; struck down, but not destroyed" (2 Corinthians 4:8, 9). Somehow, Paul handled his stress.

In the Upper Room, the cross looming on the horizon, Jesus told the disciples: "I have told you these things, so that in me you may have peace. In this world you will have trouble. But take heart! I have overcome the world" (John 16:33). The Greek word translated "trouble" means difficulty or pressure, and stress is the inevitable consequence of difficulty and pressure.

What Are The Sources Of Stress?

Dr. Jack Morris notes five major sources of stress in our society:

1. Change
2. Conflicts
3. Criticism
4. Concern—*anxiety or worry*
5. Compression

At times, more than one of these pinchers begin to get to you. You can probably relate to the following:

My job keeps me under a lot of pressure because I am in a managerial position. I have made two home moves and one office move in nine months, my boss was transferred to another department and thus I must adjust to new management. I now must supervise a full-time assistant—*for me a new experience*. I am heavily involved in my church—*often four evenings a week*—and so there have been a lot of pressures...so I worry about that, the stomach gets more upset, more worry, a vicious circle.

Coping With Stressful Events

You can't escape stress in this life. What you will usually end up doing is to move from one stressor to another, essentially trading one gunny-sack full for another. The pattern may be different, but the contents are the same. You can, however, learn to cope with it or manage it so that it doesn't do permanent damage.

Articles on stress and how to cope with it have proliferated like weeds in an unkept garden. Get on a plane and the airline magazine is almost certain to have an article for travelers on stress management. Push your grocery cart to the check stand and you are greeted with magazines with headlines in bold type that scream, "You can put stress to rest in your life!"

I've read a lot of these articles, and most of them left me with a feeling of hollowness or even frustration. Like a mother's kiss on a child's skinned knee, it may help for a bit, but the uplift is temporary and more like a desensitizer than a real cure.

It seems to me that they offer many variations on three basic themes:

1. Alter or change your perception of a stressful situation. The idea here is to help you put the situation that bothers you in perspective.

2. Practice relaxation techniques. Visualize a beautiful meadow with snow-capped mountains cresting behind and a stream meandering through the lovely flowers. Listen to soothing music. Discover deep breathing. A variety of visual stimuli all fit into this category. Get exercise—jog, swim, bicycle, walk, do aerobics. And so forth.

3. Medicate the problem. Countless tranquilizers either work on the central nervous system or allow tense muscles to relax, decreasing the level of stress.

All of the above may be helpful, but is there no more than this? Doesn't the child of God who takes the instruction of Scripture seriously have additional tools available with which he can cope with stress?

Insights From Scripture That Enable You To Fight Stress

Guideline One

Get God's perspective. It may be necessary for you to back off from the stressful situation in order to do this. Put both it and God in perspective. We are often so close to whatever is creating stress that we see neither God nor the problem in its true perspective. Stress seems to shut God out from our lives.

Go out and look at the stars on a dark night. The closest star is Alpha Centauri, 26 trillion miles out there. Light from that star, traveling at the speed of 186,400 miles per second, still takes 4.5 years to reach us. Look at the magnificent Milky Way spread across the heavens. Before God ever created the first star and put in it the sky, He knew about the stressful situation that confronts you right now. When tomorrow comes, God will be there to welcome you. Nothing takes Him by surprise.

A line in one of my computer files reads, **"REMEMBER, THIS TOO SHALL PASS...."** It is a reminder that helps me put things in their proper perspective.

Quite often we lose sight of the fact that much of what is so important today will be of little significance ten years or, perhaps, even ten days from now. We exhaust a hundred dollars of adrenaline on ten-cent events and situations with people.

I saw a sign that reads:

RULES FOR STRESS:

1. Don't sweat the small stuff.
2. It's all small stuff.

Sure, you can fight back. You can tell 'em off. You can file a grievance. You can let your temper flare and tell them where to go. Does it really matter that much?

Gaining God's perspective means you view circumstances in a different way because you are a child of God. The Bible says that nothing happens to His children as a matter of chance or fate.

Paul wrote, "In him [Christ] we were also chosen, having been predestined according to the plan of him who works out everything in conformity with the purpose of his will..." (Ephesians 1:11). To this great truth we can add the comfort of Romans 8:28: "And we know that in all things God works for the good of those who love him, who have been called according to his purpose."

The events that create stress are tools in the hands of God, and the circumstances that appear so hostile may actually be allowed by a loving God because He wants to accomplish something lasting and worthwhile that would never happen apart from your being in the pressure cooker.

One more thing must be said: there are times when this must be taken by faith. Circumstances will sometimes seem to defy this, and you'll have to tell your doubts where to get off. You will have to hold on to the truth that you know but that you may not feel. In the midst of a stressful situation, we can't see the end; only God can. However, when you are convinced that God is a good God, you can hold on and trust Him despite circumstances. That brings us to the next step.

Guideline Two

Let your relationship with God be the anchor that holds you steady in times of storm. The writer of Hebrews says that our faith is "an anchor for the soul, firm and secure" (Hebrews 6:19). The analogy is that of a ship that is not at the mercy of the storm because it is held safely by an anchor that will not fail. In the same way, the person who has the assurance that there is more to life than what he makes of it at the moment is not at the mercy of the trend in circumstances.

When you trust the Lord to bring order out of the chaos that brings stress, you will still feel the effect of the storm but you will not drift in it and be destroyed by the rocks.

God never even suggested that sufficient faith would eliminate stress in our lives. He said, "When you pass through the waters, I will be with you; and when you pass through the rivers, they will not sweep over you. When you walk through the fire, you will not be burned; the flames will not set you ablaze" (Isaiah 43:2). Notice that God never said, "If you should happen to go through the waters, fire, or flood." He said you *will* go through them, just as Jesus said, "In the world you will have trouble." The promise of His presence in times of stress becomes an anchor that gives you the strength to face the realities of life.

When you were a kid, did you ever face off with the rowdy kids in your neighborhood and exchange words? Perhaps you stood on your side of the curb and you hollered, "My daddy can beat up your daddy!" And then you probably ran for home.

Why not try that in relationship to the stressful event that has robbed you of your peace of mind? Do you believe that your Heavenly Father is sovereign Lord and God of the Universe, that He is stronger than the forces, whether evil forces or not, that have brought stress into your life? Why not hurl those words at the circumstances and then head for home? Get on your knees and remind God that you are His child and that He promised to never leave or forsake you (see Hebrews 13:5 and Matthew 28:20).

An acquaintance of mine will sometimes put his feet on his desk and say, "So what if they fire me. They can't take my family, they can't take away my wife, or my children. All they can take is my paycheck, and I'll trust God for my needs as Scripture says I can, so I'm not going to worry." He's got stress in perspective.

Guideline Three

Stop bearing your load as well as God's.

As we saw in chapter six, worry says, in effect, "God, you aren't big enough to handle this situation so I had better figure out what I'm going to do!" And worry causes stress. Do you really think that God went back to heaven, closed the door, and left you to fend for yourself? If not, then realize that there are times when you have to say, "Lord, I can't handle this. It's bigger than I am. There is absolutely nothing that I can do about it so you take over!"

Nothing creates greater frustration than not being able to solve our own problems. We are problems-solvers by nature, and we want to work out solutions. But life often presents us with circumstances that we cannot change: an illness, a difficult situation with your boss, a young adult child who seems to be making a decision he will later regret. We need to let God carry the things only He can carry.

Guideline Four

Apply Scriptural principles to the situation creating your stress.

If your stress is the result of a conflict with someone— either you have a gripe with someone or another person has something against you—you can probably relieve much of that stress by taking courage in hand and talking to the person (see Matthew 18:18:15-19 and 5:12,14). Confrontation, stressful as it may be initially, can be very positive, and it can eventually eliminate much of the turmoil you have lived with in the past.

Many times, stress is the result of sin. Affairs, dishonesty, deceit, and a host of other practices that the Bible catalogues as sin create stress—both in the life of the person who practices these things, and in the lives of those who are affected by them. "Therefore, to him who knows to do good and does not do it, to him it is sin" (James 4:17 KJV). Pretty blunt? Right!

Guideline Five

Decide what your physical and emotional load limits are. No two individuals have the same physical strength. One hunk of a man may bench press three hundred pounds, but another can't handle fifty pounds. One just happens to be born with a physique the other doesn't have. Likewise, some individuals have an amazing resiliency and can handle vast amounts of stress quite well. Others can handle very little.

175

Samuel Plimsoll (1824-1898) convinced the British Parliament to enact legislation requiring a line to be placed on the hull of every British ship. That way, the ship can only be loaded with cargo to the point where the Plimsoll line—as it came to be known—meets the water line. Loading a ship beyond that point, which had been often done by greedy ship owners, jeopardized the lives of the sailors when the ship was tossed by an angry storm. It is no wonder this gentleman was known as the sailor's friend.

But you aren't born with a Plimsoll line! Your boss can't see when you've had enough. Your husband or wife can't decide that for you. Even your doctors can't help. You are the only one in all the world who can say, "ENOUGH!" You are the only one who knows when the Plimsoll line meets the water.

Learning to say, "No!" is one of the most difficult things that we have to do. Why? Because we want to please people. We want people to like us, so we often end up saying "Yes," when we would like to say "No," but we just don't have the courage to do it.

If you have a hard time saying no, try this: "I'd like to say yes, but it's impossible. I've made a previous commitment." That *previous commitment* can be anything—your wife, your-self, or even a commitment to keep your sanity!

Guideline Six

Budget stress by managing your time. There is so much inequality in life! Whoever said life is fair? One person can eat anything he wants without gaining an ounce. The other simply walks by a bakery, smells the delicious aroma of gooey cinnamon rolls and gains weight.

But when it comes to time, every person has exactly the same quantity of it: gifted or neglected, rich or poor, young or old, in prison or free. We each have 168 hours to the week, sixty minutes to the hour.

Much of our everyday stress, though certainly not all, is the result of poor time management. We procrastinate. We put off doing the necessary. The tyranny of the urgent drains away our hours, and what we really need to accomplish never gets done.

If you need some simple help in getting a handle on your schedule, what I'm about to describe will help, provided you work at it.

Take a blank sheet of paper, or a tablet, and divide it into three columns. Label one **Must Do**, another **Should Do**, and the third **Can Do**. Under the **Must Do** heading, make a list of everything that has to be done, without fail, this week. After that, number the items—the most important one first, the next important one second, and so forth.

In the **Should Do** column, write the tasks of secondary importance, perhaps items that need to be done next week but aren't really urgent or pressing for this week. Number them in order of importance.

The **Can Do** list is made up of items that will eventually need your attention. As time passes, those items may move from column to column as they gain or lose importance.

Now, go to work on that number one item on your **Must Do** list. Though you are tempted to avoid that phone call because you don't especially want to talk to that person, don't put it off. Do the most important one first, and don't go on to the next item until you have finished that task.

Does this system work? You will be amazed how much stress you can eliminate by doing the most important task first, and then prioritizing your pressing tasks.

Guideline Seven

Be filled with the Spirit of God. Without going into a long theological discourse, let me help you see what I mean.

First of all, when you became a believer in Jesus Christ, God's Holy Spirit came to dwell in your heart and life (Romans 8:9). Paul gave us a command, a straightforward admonition to "be filled with the Spirit" (Ephesians 5:18). At the risk of over-simplifying, this means to let Jesus Christ be Lord of your life and ask Him to take control and guide you. Draw from Him the resources of grace and strength that you lack, and trust Him to work His will in your life. Know also that you are to do your part, to the extent that you know how, by following His will as it is revealed in Scripture.

Wow! All of that. Oswald Chambers put it in three words: "Let God engineer!" In other words, you willingly invite Him to take control of your life.

Paul was able to write, in his second letter to the Corinthians, "But we have this treasure in jars of clay to show that this all-surpassing power is from God and not from us. We are hard pressed on every side, but not crushed; perplexed, but not in despair; persecuted by not abandoned; struck down, but not destroyed" (2 Corinthians 4:7-9).

That's a picture of the person who faces stress—plenty of it—but is able to handle it. The secret? The indwelling presence of God's Spirit. He makes up for what you lack.

Let's use Paul's metaphor. Picture three vases: One is made of clay; another is made of marble, which is stronger; and the third is made of metal, which is stronger still. Obviously, their ability to withstand stress is in increasing order. Now, in your mind's eye, picture a strong hand inside the weaker vases. That hand will equalize their strength. It gives each vase the same ability to withstand pressure from without. That is exactly what the Holy Spirit does in each of our lives.

When I was a boy, I remember visiting Van Briggle Pottery in Colorado Springs. I watched with interest as the old potter took a lump of clay and kneaded it with his hand, molding and shaping the lump. Then, he put it on the potter's wheel as he began working the treadle with his foot.

From this amorphous lump of clay, the shape of a vessel slowly began to emerge. Carefully, the potter placed one hand within the vessel and with the other hand applied pressure without in order to shape the vessel he was making.

The hand of God is within you, and it supports you much like the potter supports the clay as he molds it. From without, the strong hand of the Almighty insures that nothing beyond His power will ever confront you.

His strength within you is more than equal to the stress that is without.

Discussion Questions:

Three young executives on Wall Street were tired of the stress and pressure they experienced in the New York brokerage firm where they all worked. They decided to liquidate their assets, buy a sailboat and relax as they sailed around the world.

It was a great idea! They equipped the sailboat and began their journey. In a few months they sailed into one of the most beautiful lagoons they had ever seen. Miles of beautiful, undulating sandy beaches, clear blue water, beautiful coral reefs, and warm, romantic breezes.

"What a magnificent place for a resort!" one of them commented after a few days of enjoying the scenic beauty.

"Yeah, that's what I've been thinking," replied a second.

In due time, they decided to stay and build that resort. A local contractor was hired, but he worked on a native schedule, not on a Western one. Materials couldn't be located, deadlines were ignored, and when it finally opened, the local employees were lax about being on time or simply didn't show up when they didn't want to. And nobody seemed upset by any of it, apart from the three men who wanted to put the resort together.

1. What might the three men have done to cope with stress in the brokerage firm instead of running from it? How might they manage the stress of the new situation?

2. Think of a time when you were under a lot of stress. What effects did it have on you and in your life? How did you manage—or not manage—the pressure and its impact?

3. What are three good stresses in your life? What are three bad stresses? What steps can you take today to keep those things in balance instead of letting them overwhelm you?

This will hurt....

Sometimes we think that being under stress means that we settle in for the long haul and keep pushing through. It will hurt if you think of taking breaks as *weakness*. It will hurt to convince yourself that you can rest later—after the deadline is met, after the kids are grown, on the weekend, when you retire.

This will help....

Evaluate whether the stress you are facing is the positive kind that helps motivate you to accomplish things or is the negative kind that pulverizes your productivity. Learn to work *smarter*, not *harder*, whether the task is cleaning the house or winning an account. We all need to take care of ourselves physically, emotionally, and spiritually. It will help to consciously focus on ways to do that each day.

CHAPTER TEN

Burn-Out:

Terminal stress

for generations, parents told their children, "Nobody ever died from hard work; now get out there and go to work!" But that is no longer true. Behavioral scientists began using a term to describe people that was formerly used of engines that had exhausted their fuel: BURN-OUT. Burn-out is what happens when a person works too hard under too much stress for too long a period of time. That causes him to lose his equilibrium.

Dr. Carolyn Karr, Associate Professor of Social Studies at Marshall University, writes:

> There are more people in danger of succumbing to the burn-out syndrome than in any period in our history. The reasons are quite simple: There are more people working; there is greater competition for existing jobs; and inflation is placing tremendous pressure on people to keep the jobs they now have.[1]

What Kind Of People Burn Out?

The people who are especially vulnerable to burn-out are those in highly stressful situations. Burn-out applies to people who once loved their work but who are now overwhelmed by it. They do not cope effectively any longer. It's not that they can't—it's just that they have lost their desire to cope. Burn-out is the most severe form of stress, and it can be terminal.

Any situation in which constant demands are made on a person is a highly stressful situation. Schedules become busier and busier, and a person's life might take on the appearance of a well-worn rut. The most susceptible individuals are professionals such as counselors, nurses, doctors, teachers, lawyers, scientists, ministers and missionaries.

The formula for burn-out is simple:

$$\frac{\text{PEOPLE-TO-PEOPLE}}{\text{CONTACT}} + \text{STRESS} = \text{BURN-OUT}$$

According to Herbert J. Freudenberger, a New York psychoanalyst, certain personality types are more prone to burn-out than others. They are:

1. The person who needs to succeed and to feel successful. Often this person has come from a rather insignificant social background. Maybe he has risen through the ranks from the bottom. He may be from a very poor family, and becoming a person of status is very important to him. This person doesn't view success as the only thing in life, but he thinks it's way ahead of whatever is in second place. In short, winning is the name of the game for this type of person; it is the only thing that really counts.

2. The over-committed individual. Ministers, missionaries, and church workers step to the front in this category. Does that mean that their commitment to Christ is too great? No, but it might mean that their commitment to His work is, and that they have difficulty distinguishing between the two. Bearing loads of responsibility that God never intended them to bear, they eventually want to walk away from the whole thing, "throwing the baby out with the bath water," as it were.

3. The extremely competent individual. This type of person thinks that he is the only one capable of handling the job. Although this person may not voice it, you get the feeling that the individual considers himself indispensable, that the whole operation will collapse unless he is there eighteen hours a day. This person has usually never learned to delegate responsibility, and when he does he often ends up taking back the very task he assigned to someone else. When this pattern is at work, there is a burn-out candidate in the making.

Burn-Out: A New Outbreak Of An Old Disease

Burn-out isn't new. You can read about it in the pages of the Bible. Men such as Jonah and Elijah were confronted with it. I think we face it in greater measure today, however. People who should by all rights be productive become warped, weary and—well, burnt out.

It may help you avoid the fate yourself if you understand the symptoms and the stages of the burn-out process.

What Are The Symptoms?

Again, the symptoms of burn-out will affect all three of the areas that make up the composite of our lives: physical, emotional, and spiritual. Although the three cannot be separated into neat little compartments, there are, nonetheless, very definite symptoms in each.

Physical Symptoms

Physical weariness is one of the most prominent symptoms. When you are faced with burn-out, you are tired all the time. You go to bed tired, you get up tired, you run tired all day. In fact, you even sleep tired, and you can't quite shake it. You traipse from meeting to meeting, from appointment to appointment. You'd really like to stop the world and get off, but you just don't have that option.

You may also suffer any combination of the following: headache, gastrointestinal problems, weight fluctuation—generally weight loss, but it can be the opposite—insomnia, hypertension, and even chest pains. These are not imagined symptoms; they are very real. Like the engine that has exhausted its fuel, you are rapidly exhausting the physical and emotional resources that make your life vibrant and meaningful.

Emotional Symptoms

Burn-out causes dramatic changes in personality. Outgoing, extroverted people who customarily make significant contributions to meetings and in discussion with their associates can become quiet, sullen, and even withdrawn. The burn-out candidate who used to have energy for romps with the kids and household chores at home is listless and lethargic. He's lost interest in everything. A person who has been pretty much *under-control* becomes irritable and often hostile. He may be depressed. He tends to be rigid and wants to make no changes. Any questions is interpreted as a challenge, and any suggestion is considered insubordination.

Spiritual Symptoms

The burn-out candidate feels that God has become remote, disinterested, and withdrawn. He becomes critical of fellow Christians. He loses interest in the Bible, and when he does read it, it makes little sense. Church attendance becomes perfunctory, if he even continues to go. When he does attend, he doesn't see much right with the service anyway.

The Four Phases Of The Burn-Out Process

As I see it, there are four phases to the burn-out cycle. I have seen these phases time and time again in my colleagues and as I counsel others. These phases and their characteristics are:

CHALLENGE
> Goal-oriented
> High expectations
> Idealistic
> Achiever

COMMITMENT
> Life still adventurous
> Thrill of the kill
> Building
> Productive
> Achieving

CONTAINMENT

Indifferent

Workaholic

Pursued by goals

Driven

Not appreciated

Perspective warped

COLLAPSE

Overwhelmed

Quits or escapes

May use drugs, sex, alcohol

Broken relationship or fellowship with God

The first two phases are not dangerous. They are the part of the cycle that falls within having a vital and productive life. The second two stages, however, are damaging. When a person begins any new thing in life, he is usually excited about the possibilities in front of him. He is full of idealism and eager to pour himself into the task.

As time goes on, a person passes into the second phase. This, too, is generally a productive stage. Life hasn't lost its glamour and the person is still reaching forward in a spirit of adventure. It is at this point that things become dangerous if stress is not handled well. This second stage can rapidly become routine and perfunctory.

Phase number three is a dangerous one. That's when a person is no longer pursuing his goals; rather, his goals pursue him. "We are driven," a Nissan commercial says, and so is the individual who is at this stage in the burn-out cycle. He is not quite out of the game, but he is only one short step away, like when there are two strikes against the batter and the pitcher is winding up with a fast ball. This person feels unappreciated. He develops a martyr complex. He can relate to the saying, "The hurrieder I go, the behinder I get"; he feels like he just can't get on top of things. He may end up hurting the very people he wants to help.

An article in a nursing magazine summed up the situation in that context:

> You entered nursing to help people...to do good for humanity...then one day, you're ashamed because you yelled at a patient. On another day you cry over the cruelty of death. You slip into days of avoiding patients...or even making fun of patients' personalities or illness. You begin to dread work. You become cynical—and you're ashamed of yourself for feeling that way. You become disgusted.[2]

One morning, the burnt out person wakes up and says to himself, "Is this all there is to life? It just isn't worth it!" The trap has sprung! He's in the fourth stage of the cycle. He may simply walk out, slam the door on life, quit. He is overwhelmed by what should have been a good and proper experience. He wants to escape; drugs, alcohol, even sexual encounters are enticing. Those who are closest to the person are usually the ones hurt in the explosion. Relationships are almost always disturbed or broken.

When I recently did a series of programs about burn-out on my radio broadcast, we received the greatest deluge of mail that has ever come to our office (with the possible exception of a series on depression). One woman described phase four in these words:

> My husband got up from the dinner table one Sunday evening in January, and left us. He sounds so much like the person you described in your three programs this

week. There isn't anything I can do about him because I don't know where he is.

The following are also very typical of the letters we received:

Your description of the burn-out victim sounds exactly like my wife who works as an assistant manager in a bank.... In fact, she suffers from every one you mentioned.

I've come to the shocking realization that you have depicted my life to a tee. My wife is a reading consultant for neurologically impaired children while I am a communications manager for a large company. Both of us have had it!

The Burn-Out Candidate Forgets Some Very Important Things

1. Even spiritual giants burn out. You can read in the Bible of Elijah's traumatic *burn-out*. Here was a prophet who single-handedly confronted the 450 prophets of Baal (1 Kings 18, 19), but the emotional and physical drain resulting from that confrontation brought him to the brink of burn-out. When he was challenged by Jezebel—the original *women's libber*, he gave in to the exhaustion, and he turned and fled for his life. The life of Elijah reminds us that even spiritual giants get tired and discouraged. Even the most godly people are prime candidates for burn-out.

2. Even nature teaches the importance of restoration. A period of rest and restoration always follow the harvest. Winter

always follows Autumn. This is God's way of allowing the land to refurbish itself. Constant production without restoration depletes the natural resources and diminishes the quality of produce.

3. Jesus and all of Scripture clearly teach that rest is critical. When the seventy who had been commissions by Jesus to minister in nearby cities returned, Jesus instructed, "Come apart and rest a while."

And the Apostle Paul recognized that burn-out is a vital threat to those involved in people-to-people ministries. He instructed, "Let us not become weary in doing good, for at the proper time we will reap a harvest if we do not give up" (Galatians 6:9). The King James Bible puts it a bit more succinctly: "We shall reap in due season if we faint not." In today's language, Paul would say, "We will reap in due season if we don't burn out first."

4. God thinks that what we are is more important than what we do. Having lost sight of God's perspective, the burn-out candidate feels that accomplishment is the only thing that counts. He usually places greater value on his goals than on people, so reaching his objective is the only thing that matters. The goal may be a good one in and of itself; the problem is with how the goal is accomplished.

When a person faces burn-out, no matter what field he's in, that person's family is always affected. More times than not, his marriage is seriously threatened in the process. A person can be the finest missionary statesman there is. He can leave behind a great organization and a legacy of admirable benevolence. But if he burns out in the process, if his family has to pay the price, it's not worth it. If you can head burn-out off at the pass, the later years of your life will be happier and far more productive.

"It is better to burn-out than to rust-out," some people say. In one sense, they may be right. But I don't believe we're choosing between the lesser of two evils. I don't think God would have us do either. The Bible describes ways that we can reach our goals without burning out.

How To Avoid Burn-Out And Reach Your Goals

Guideline One

Get your perspective right. Jesus did not heal everyone in Palestine when He was here on earth. Undoubtedly, there were many people within easy walking distance who had needs, deep needs, and Jesus didn't get over there to minister to them. There were limitations to what He could accomplish in the natural world while still maintaining His spiritual life.

You can't bear the burdens of the entire world, or even your own city. Therefore, if you are to avoid burn-out, you have to bring your priorities into subjection to the will of your Heavenly Father. What is it that God wants you to do? When you take more upon your shoulders than God intended you to, you will spread yourself too thin and some of your tasks will not be done as well as they could have been.

Guideline Two

Take time off. To avoid burn-out, you must learn to take time off for rest and recuperation. That includes spiritual recuperation as well. "There is no music in a rest," wrote a famous composer, "but, there is the making of it." When you think that things will simply collapse if you take time off or go away for a vacation, you could be in the containment phase of the burn-out cycle. If that is true, you are literally on the brink of collapse.

My guess is that Jesus did not get away to the mountains or the desert for fun and frolic. He went primarily for prayer and rest. He went to recoup His emotional and spiritual resources, to ponder the will of His Father, to maintain His equilibrium so that He could minister productively in the power of the Spirit when He returned.

Guideline Three

Start taking care of yourself physically. This doesn't mean that you should stand in front of the mirror longer, applying your makeup or combing your thinning hair. What it does mean is that you need to stop neglecting your body. Most people who are on the verge of burn-out have been so busy that they have no time for tennis, jogging, or any other physical exercise. They are usually overweight. Instead of exercise, they turn to the refrigerator. They run up a flight of stairs and are out of breath for an hour.

Your body is the temple of the Holy Spirit, and you need to start taking care of it. This involves a combination of proper diet, exercise, and recreation. You're not a machine that can be programmed; you are a person created in the image of God. You have a human body, which is God's property, and it must be given proper care.

Guideline Four

Learn to say, "No." Life is a matter of choices. Not all of those choices are between good and bad. Each of us must evaluate several good things and then choose the best. Sometimes those choices are difficult.

We discussed a personality type earlier in the chapter, a person who has to do everything himself. This person, in the early stages of the game, may think that there are two kinds of people—the willing and the able. But, he believes, the willing are too often not able, and the able are too often not willing.

This burn-out candidate takes on more and more by himself, to insure that the job gets done and his objectives are accomplished. After all, the needs that he's meeting are real, and "no" is a word he never learned.

Any person, however, needs to know when to use that word, whether he is the type who cannot delegate or not. Good is the enemy of the best. We all need to learn to say more often, "I would very much like to take on that responsibility, but with my present commitments, it is impossible. Thank you very much, but my answer is 'no.'"

Guideline Five

Delegate responsibility. This means at home as well as at the office. Maybe you can do the job better than the person to whom you delegate the task; that's probably why you are in charge. But being in charge also means being able to delegate, and being able to delegate means yielding authority to the other person so that he can get the job done.

Once you've delegated something, turn loose. In the words of Dwight L. Moody, "The successful man isn't the man who does the work of ten men, but the man who gets ten men to do the work."

Guideline Six

Learn the secret of spiritual renewal. We've already established that burn-out affects your spiritual life as well as your emotional life. You will find your relationship with God strained and under stress. Part of the reason for this is that you don't have time for Him, just as you have had no time for your family. When you read the Word, you may not be able to get much out of it because you can't quiet your mind and keep your thoughts on what you are reading. Since it feels like a waste of time anyway, you push the Word aside or fall asleep as you read. You feel like giving up spiritually just as you feel like giving up on your job, your ministry, or your family. You are definitely burning out!

If there is a secret to spiritual survival, it is this: our relationship to God through Jesus Christ must be sustained on a daily basis. Relationship is never a one-shot-for-life sort of thing, and our relationship with Jesus is no different in that respect. Paul wrote, "Therefore we do not lose heart. Though outwardly we are wasting away, *yet inwardly we are being renewed day by day*" (2 Corinthians 4:16, emphasis mine).

Daily renewal involves quiet time with God. I find that it works best to start your day reading His Word and opening your heart to Him in prayer. When I get to the place where reading the Word is mechanical, when I go through the motions but don't get anything out of it, or when I pray and it seems that the heavens are brass, I recognize this as a danger signal. It is a red light flashing on the instrument panel of life that says, "You're going too fast, man, slow down!"

What's The Answer?

Suppose that you are driving down the highway in your automobile and the red light on your instrument panel indicates that your oil pressure is down. The engine still sounds good. When you gun the throttle, it responds normally. What do you do? You can either ignore the light and continue driving, or you can pull over and investigate so you can determine what is wrong. Even if you choose to ignore the warning light, your automobile will continue to perform for a while, just as it always has. But then, it will burn out. Then, you'll be dead in your tracks! Finished!

What do you do when you see the signals, the warning indications that you have moved from the commitment stage of life to the containment stage? Do you ignore them, or do you do something about them? Friend, it is one thing to recognize the symptoms; it is another thing to know what to do about them. But it is another matter entirely to be motivated enough to take action, to come to a place where you say, "I will do something about my life to insure that I don't become a burn-out victim!" Again, your wife can't do it for you; your husband can't do it for you. Only you can.

I delivered a series of lectures in Australia that focused on the problem of burn-out among professionals involved in Christian work. A participant at the conference came to me afterwards and said, "There is one more stage to the burn-out cycle that you have overlooked!"

"What is that?" I asked.

"It is the *come-back*," replied the friend.

He's absolutely right! Individuals who have already burned out don't have to quit forever, and they don't have to use burn-out as a rationale to excuse their behavior. Through restoration and healing, there is a way out of collapse.

One woman described her come-back like this:

About three years ago I experienced burn-out myself and am just now putting myself back together. My husband and I came very close to becoming separated...but something beautiful has come of it. With three children, ages thirteen, eleven, and two, I am very glad, with the enormous help of God, we put things back together again. Your program and tapes have been a great deal responsible for our marriage and sanity's survival.

The habits and patterns that led to burn-out in the first place will challenge restoration and healing, but you can come back. As you begin to reverse some of those well-worn habits, the inner struggles that have torn apart the fabric of your life will begin to subside, and peace will flood your heart. It is well worth the sacrifice and determination. When you are challenged with burn-out, remember, you **CAN** make a come-back.

Discussion Questions:

Brad graduated with an MBA, one of the top students in his graduating class. He started climbing the corporate ladder, and became just as successful in his profession as he was in school. He has all of the toys that go along with success—the BMW, the Rolex, a membership in an elite country club—and all the earmarks of a man who is going somewhere. He also has a wife and two young boys, and is on four committees at church—one of which he is the chairman. He feels good about his life, but he is tired a lot of the time and evening meetings cause him to miss his sons' baseball games more often. Recently, he has been skipping lunch because he doesn't feel like eating, and muscle spasms in his lower back are getting to be more than occasional.

1. What are some of the obvious signs that Brad may be a burn-out candidate? Each person can handle a different amount of stress and number of commitments. If Brad wants to maintain a very high level of quality activity, what are some things he needs to put into practice?

2. Hard work is a good thing. What was one time when you let hard work get out of balance? How did you bring it back into balance so that it was a creative instead of a destructive force in your life?

3. Consider the four phases of the burn-out cycle: Challenge, commitment, containment and collapse. Which phase are you in—at work, at home, personally? What are some things you can do today to move into the come-back stage?

4. We have discussed a number of inner struggles in this book. What is another inner struggle that you have that we did not talk about? How might you use some of the information in this book to win that struggle?

This will hurt....

Many people believe that the only way to have the lifestyle they want is to give in to excessive hard work. It will hurt if you justify your choices based on material rewards. A BMW, as too many people find out, will not keep a marriage together. It will hurt to keep pushing, driven by the sense that *making it big* is a demonstration of your worth. It will hurt to ignore the red lights on the dashboard of your life.

This will help....

Know yourself (chapter one) and what characteristics contribute to your being a candidate for burn-out. It will help to set your priorities so that you can balance all of your responsibilities. Occasionally, give yourself permission to let something fall by the wayside—without feeling guilty!

Notes

[1]Carolyn Karr as quoted by Donna Sammons, "Burn-out," Family Weekly, March 9, 1980, p. 15.

[2]Cheryl Pilate, "People-orientated Professionals Risk Burnout," Register, February 26, 1981, section E, p. 11.

grandfather who saw considerable action in the war would sit out on the porch with his grandsons and entertain them with stories of his valor. One warm Sunday afternoon, he recounted one of his favorite stories. He had carried the flag for his regiment and, though the bullets were flying all around him, he gained the crest of the hill and proudly planted the flag in full view of the enemy.

After he finished the story, he sat back, expecting the children to say, "Hey, that was great, Grandpa; tell us another story." Instead one of the boys asked pensively, "But Grandpa, what happened?"

That's the question I want to leave with you as we come to the end of our discussion on winning your inner struggles. What is going to be different in your life as the result of reading this book? What decisions have you made that must be executed? Where do you go from here?

You are the one who holds the answer. Today can be different from yesterday because God is the God of the present. He wants to meet you at the point of your deepest need.

I have not even begun to deal with all the inner struggles that confront us. I have simply touched on some of the most prevalent. Men and women will continue to wage battles with these inner forces that destroy their peace of mind and create turmoil in their lives. I am absolutely convinced, however, that much of what robs us of peace and wholeness is contrary to God's plan and purpose for our lives. You can win over those inner struggles that threaten to defeat you, and you can unlock your potential to be all that God created you to be. May God help you to do so!

If I can be of personal help, I would be happy to hear from you. You can write to me at the following addresses:

In the United States:
   Guidelines
   Box G
   Laguna Hills, CA 92654

In Asia:
   Guidelines
   Box 2041
   Manila, Philippines